Moral Hazard in American Healthcare

GARY FRADIN

MORAL HAZARD IN AMERICAN HEALTHCARE
WHY WE CAN'T CONTROL OUR MEDICAL EXPENSES

2007

Moral Hazard in American Healthcare

TABLE OF CONTENTS

ACKNOWLEDGEMENTS

I wrote this book to help clarify many healthcare economic ideas to myself.

From my student days at Lancaster, London and Harvard Universities and continuing through my business career, I have been interested in the underlying economic factors that influence human behavior. Which groups, I wondered, benefit most from our current healthcare system? How does our healthcare finance system reward and maintain the status quo? What economic incentives exist in alternate healthcare proposals? Do we get good value for our healthcare investments?

Writing this book afforded me the opportunity to research, consider and clarify some basic healthcare economic issues to myself.

Many people helped in this thinking and writing process. I would particularly like to thank Dr. Michael Gordon, Dr. Norman Weinstein, Michael Lesser, Charlie Banner, Christopher Wilson, Dr. Herbert Keyser, Bob Was, Richard Capobianco, Jeff Rich, Ed Barulli, Fran Nagle and Michelle Spaulding. My entire customer base asked insightful questions and provided quality input. As I taught seminars on these various topics, numerous students asked excellent questions, made pointed comments and helped focus my thinking.

And this book would never have been completed without the love and support from my wife Marjorie and sons Ben and Isaac.

PREFACE

This short introduction to American healthcare finance addresses three primary questions: first, 'why is American healthcare so expensive', second 'why do health insurance premiums inflate faster than other American goods and services', and third 'why are Americans no healthier than other people'?

I answer these questions by reviewing various types of health insurance—indemnity, managed care, health savings accounts, association health plans and single payer systems. For indemnity and managed care insurance, I look primarily at cost and quality control mechanisms employed by American carriers during the past 30 years. For health savings accounts, association health plans and single payer systems, I first explain the theory and practice of each in moderate detail before considering if these are improvements over our existing system.

This book argues that the current American healthcare system works reasonably well for many groups—Medicare beneficiaries, sick people, employees, doctors, hospitals and insurance companies among others. Though many businesses and consumers complain about high health insurance premiums, other groups are sufficiently satisfied with our current healthcare finance system to continue supporting it.

Specifically, I argue that American healthcare consumers value freedom of choice among providers and treatments more highly than they do low health insurance premiums. I also argue that American healthcare providers—physicians and hospitals—strongly resist outside interference in the doctor/patient relationship. These two forces make the American healthcare system extraordinarily difficult to control.

I wrote this book for three audiences. First, I aim at the 'generally interested' population concerned about high healthcare premiums. This group is my insurance agency's customers—small business owners, self-employed folks and middle income employees—who struggle to pay health insurance premiums. These people ask 'why is my health insurance so expensive' and often believe that 'they' should do something about it (without specifying exactly who 'they' are). I try to show this group some of the cost and quality control programs that various healthcare finance systems employ…and why many don't work.

Second, I aim to inform healthcare finance professionals—insurance brokers, hospital administrators, insurance carrier managers among others—about these issues. Brokers, I believe, have a responsibility to educate their clients who quite reasonably want to understand why their premiums rise every year. We regularly hear 'My premiums increased by 10%, and I didn't even visit the doctor last year. Why?' Most health insurance brokers are quite good at explaining insurance regulations and carrier underwriting requirements—but relatively poor at explaining the underlying economic issues.

Hospital and insurance managers also regularly interact with their paying customers and share this education responsibility.

Third, I aim at healthcare administration students—people who will be working in the healthcare field shortly. I tried to discuss real world healthcare finance issues—the kind that will engage students in their professional lives. Healthcare graduates may be asked their opinion of association health plans, or whether a single payer system is more attractive than Health Savings Accounts, or why our healthcare system is so expensive. I hope this books helps them construct reasonable answers.

My own experience as a health insurance broker has highlighted the importance of customer education. I have consistently found that explaining healthcare economics to clients pleases them and makes them more comfortable with their policies. Short explanations often lead to a long ones as clients ask follow-up question after follow-up question—generally with the preface 'Can I ask you just one more question?'. Healthcare consumers, in my experience, really want to understand both the strengths and weaknesses of our healthcare system.

I believe that heightening the overall understanding of US healthcare economics among health insurance professionals will help us educate our clients and raise the level of debate in this country.

I hope the reader will find that reading this book is a useful experience.

INTRODUCTION
MORAL HAZARD IDENTIFIED

The US healthcare system is enormous and confusing. We currently spend over 15% of our GDP on healthcare with that projected to hit almost 19% by 2014. (1)

This compares to Switzerland and Germany that spend approximately 11% of their GDP on healthcare, France and Canada that spend about 10%, Sweden, Holland, Denmark and Italy that spend about 9%, and Britain that spends about 8% (2).

US per capita healthcare spending in 2002 was $5,267 compared to the $2,049 average of other developed countries. Switzerland had the second highest average per capital spending at $3,446—less than 2/3 of the US amount.

Our total healthcare expenditures have grown from about $27 billion in 1960 to almost $2 trillion ($2,000 billion) in 2006.

What have we purchased?

Our life expectancy at birth in 2001 (77.5 years) was lower than Japan (81.5), Australia (80) or Britain (79) (3).

Our infant mortality rate of 6.9 deaths/1000 live births exceeded Britains of 5.3, as did our obesity rate of 30.6% compared to Britains 22%. (4)

Yet we have more MRI machines per capita (8.1 per million population) than Australia (4.7), Britain (3.9), France (2.8) or Canada (2.5). (5)

We perform more Coronary Angioplasty procedures per capita (388 per 100,000 of population) than Germany (165), Denmark (82), Canada (80), New Zealand (65) or Britain (51), and more Coronary Bypass procedures (203 per 100,000 population) than Britain (41) or Canada (65). (6)

And we consume more pharmaceuticals ($556/capita) than any other country in the world—by almost 20% more than France (#2 in the world). (7)

In spite of our extraordinary level of healthcare expenditures, some 45 million Americans lack basic health insurance and receive little (if any) preventive care.

Nonetheless, we <u>feel</u> better than others. The Organization for Economic Cooperation and Development (OECD) reported in 2002 that 85% of Americans between ages 45 and 64 reported their health as 'Good', compared to 84% of Canadians, 74% of Danes, 71% of Britons and 58% of Germans. (8)

How can we understand this? We spend more money on healthcare than any other country but live less long. We have more technology than others but higher infant mortality rates. We're more obese but feel better. What common element underlies these apparent contradictions—and what problem should we Americans focus on solving?

This book argues that the problem underlying our high cost / low quality healthcare system is Moral Hazard. Moral hazard is an economic term that describes how behavior changes when an insurance company pays.

The moral hazard concept originated when fire industry executives became concerned that people with 'poor moral character' might purchase policies and then burn down their own houses to collect the insurance proceeds. Such people might even 'over-insure' their houses to make a profit on the enterprise—and drive up premiums for everyone.

Flood insurance companies worry that insured homeowners might build in flood plains—figuring that the insurance company would pay to rebuild should a flood occur. Auto insurance carriers concern themselves with policyholders who intentionally cause auto accidents to gain insurance benefits. And health carriers worry that people will have expensive, unnecessary medical tests and procedures when their out-of-pocket costs are negligible.

Moral hazard is an elusive, difficult to grasp concept. Much like pornography, it's hard to define but recognizable upon sight. Moral hazard is healthcare systemic inefficiency. We'll use three definitions.

First, healthcare <u>efficiency</u> means 'having the patient get care that is worth at least what it costs, but get no care that is worth less than what it costs'. Moral hazard is the opposite: patients may get care worth less (in terms of longevity gains or life quality improvements) than the costs.

Second, healthcare efficiency is 'the treatment plan that your primary care physician, who is well versed in the current medical literature and knows your medical condition would approve, absent any economic considerations.' Moral hazard is the opposite—a treatment plan that includes economic considerations. A patient might say 'I don't know if I really need this test or procedure, but maybe I do and it's free (to me), so I might as well have it.' A provider might say 'I don't know if the patient really needs this test or procedure, but it may provide some benefit, it's free (to them) and I can bill the insurance carrier, so I might as well do it.'

Third, healthcare efficiency means 'getting the maximum treatment benefit at the lowest cost'. When moral hazard enters the picture providers might recommend beneficial but costly treatments and ignore equally (or more) beneficial but less expensive remedies.

Why might a patient receive more expensive than necessary treatments, or care worth less than what it costs? George Bernard Shaw figured this out in <u>The Doctor's Dilemma</u> in 1911: 'That any sane nation, having observed that you could provide for the supply of bread by giving bakers a (financial) interest in baking for you, should go on to give a surgeon a (financial) interest in cutting off your leg, is enough to make one despair'.

Under most insurance payment programs providers receive 'fee-for-service' payments, often calculated as 'cost-plus reimbursement'. Physicians only get paid if they perform a service. Hospitals get paid only if they treat. The physician or hospital has a financial interest to treat and earns the most by providing the most expensive treatment. Meanwhile the patient has little or no <u>financial</u> interest in receiving low cost treatment or avoiding treatment altogether.

In addition to promoting healthcare inefficiency, moral hazard also causes inequity in our healthcare system. Inequity occurs when some people use more than their required (fair) share of medical resources. This raises premiums to all others and, frighteningly, provides an inducement for some people to demand even <u>more</u> medical services. 'She has an MRI whenever she has a headache', so goes the rationale, 'so I think I will too. After all, I've been paying my premiums and I might as well get some benefits.'

Jonathan Skinner, a Dartmouth healthcare economist summarizes moral hazard problems: 'On equity grounds, we have problems with the idea of single working mothers in Nebraska (often themselves lacking health insurance) footing the bill for gold-plated health care provided to high-income Medicare enrollees. Leaving equity aside, on efficiency grounds, why should Medicare continue to pay billions of dollars every year on health care that does nothing for longevity, nothing for patient satisfaction and nothing for better access to care?' (9)

Our cost gatekeepers—Primary Care Physicians—exacerbate this problem under the guise of 'defensive medicine' or 'ruling out' a potential medical problem. PCPs quite correctly often fear lawsuits if they miss something. Why not order an extra MRI, chest x-ray or blood test, if only to demonstrate that you've done everything reasonable to diagnose the problem?

This book will explore moral hazard in American healthcare. Chapter 1 discusses why healthcare is different from other types of economic activity, making the potential for moral hazard so profound. Chapter 2 discusses moral hazard under traditional indemnity plans—the coverage most Americans had until about 1990. Chapter 3 discusses moral hazard under managed care—the type of coverage most Americans have had since the 1990s. Chapter 4 looks at President Bush's attempts to improve healthcare, Health Savings Accounts and Association Health Plans. Chapter 5 looks at how Single Payer Systems deal with these issues: we use the British National Health Service as an example. Chapter 6 asks if we get a reasonable economic return for our healthcare investment in spite of the moral hazard inefficiencies.

And Chapter 7 offers some hope for positive changes in the future.

As I wrote this book, I kept reminding myself that—for all it's flaws and problems—the US healthcare system provides our insured population with an outstanding product. We have access to the newest technologies, choice among very good hospitals, an abundance of highly trained specialists and relatively short waits for treatment. I see moral hazard as a problem needing solution, rather than a cancer that will destroy our medical system. And I see the American healthcare system as sufficiently vibrant and dynamic to control moral hazard and improve itself over time.

I also compare our healthcare system to Winston Churchill's pithy summary of democracy. 'Democracy', said Sir Winston, 'is the worst form of government, except for all the others.'

The same applies to our healthcare system.

Introduction: Notes

1. Projected by Medicare and reported in USA Today, 3/2/05.
2. All GDP rates are 2002 figures produced by the Organization for Economic Cooperation and Development and published in 2004 as Health Data.
3. 'Keep Taking the Medicine' The Economist, July 15, 2004
4. OECD Health Data, 2006
5. Gerard F. Anderson, et al. 'It's the Prices, Stupid: Why the United States Is So Different from Other Countries,' Health Affairs, Vol. 22, No. 3, May/June 2003
6. Ibid.
7. Ibid.
8. OECD Health Data, 2004—data from 1998- 2000
9. Quoted in Maggie Mahar, 'Money Driven Medicine' Collins, 2006, page 168

CHAPTER 1
Unique features of the healthcare marketplace

The market for healthcare products and services differs from other types of economic activities in several fundamental ways. This chapter will explore some unique aspects of the healthcare economy to understand why moral hazard plays such a significant role.

THE TYPICAL MARKET ECONOMY

In our consumer-oriented economy, buyers typically have **good access to information** about the products or services they purchase. Buyers can research products and services, see these products in action or talk to people who have purchased similar services. Marketers and advertisers will point out advantages of certain products and disadvantages of others. Products that consumers don't like disappear fairly quickly from the marketplace.

With typical consumer goods—a car for example—buyers gain experience purchasing over time. This affords an opportunity to learn from mistakes and to select a future car that offers features you wish you had purchased last time. Typically, you take a 'consultant' (a parent or more experienced friend) to help purchase your first car—and then a few years later have the experience and confidence to purchase on your own. Economists call this 'experience learning'.

When purchasing a car, you may want to analyze comparative information. You may wish to compare sizes, power or feel—all easily done in a test drive. You may wish to compare fuel efficiency or safety ratings—information very easily obtained. You may wish to see which cars are most popular, which you can do simply by driving around and looking. You may wish to find a good, reputable dealer with which you feel comfortable—again, easy to do, perhaps by asking friends or talking to the dealer.

Information—the basis of any reasonable purchasing decision—is typically readily available for the standard goods that most Americans consume.

A key aspect of product and service buying information is **price**. Our economy typically defines price as 'what a willing buyer will pay and what a willing seller will accept'. When a supplier has too many products in inventory, he reduces prices; or when consumers demand more of a service than is readily available, suppliers raise prices. Price helps define the interaction of supply and demand for a specific product or service.

Consumers also—generally implicitly—understand the **quantifiable risk of poor purchasing decisions**. If your car doesn't work within X days of purchase, you can return it under 'Lemon Law' regulations. If you change your mind about your car's color, you can repaint it. If you need a better radio, you can upgrade. If you simply have buyer's remorse you can resell your car, though probably at a financial loss.

Your potential losses from typical consumer purchases are generally limited to a percentage of the purchase price; you cannot lose your life, end up in pain or become an invalid from a poor purchase. These risk limits play an important role in understanding differences between the healthcare market and other economic markets. Only in the healthcare market can purchase options literally feel like 'life and death' decisions—whether or not they really are. This heightened perceived risk plays a key role in understanding healthcare purchase decisions.

HOW THE HEALTHCARE MARKET DIFFERS FROM TYPICAL ECONOMIC MARKETS

Purchase decisions in the healthcare market differ from our paradigm 'normal economic market' in terms of **information, risk** and **price**.

Healthcare consumers rarely (hopefully) make repetitive large healthcare purchases. Most people never shop for pediatric neurological services, so have no background or experience buying such a product. Unlike our car example, people even more rarely shop for a <u>second</u> pediatric neurologist, so have no ability to use their experience from purchasing their first pediatric neurological services as a basis for purchasing their second.

Economists call this 'irregular and unpredictable purchasing'. People rarely buy the same complex medical services regularly over time so have very little first-hand experience upon which to base their specialist consumption decisions.

Further, no two patient experiences or medical conditions are exactly alike. This reduces the utility of relying on friend's recommendations. Your child's neurological issues may differ significantly from your friend's child (assuming you can even find a friend with experience purchasing pediatric neurological services), so your friend's advice may well be worthless. This problem is called 'idiosyncratic purchasing'—i.e. your case is unique.

People purchasing irregularly, unpredictably and idiosyncratically face two other significant informational problems when purchasing medical care. First, these medical decisions (often) must be made quickly. Second, these decisions are often made while the consumer feels ill. Both of these factors combine to increase the (perceived) risk of poor decision making.

We generally make medical consumption decisions quickly either because we have an acute illness needing immediate treatment, or because we <u>worry</u> that we have a potentially acute illness. Human beings dislike uncertainty and often want a diagnosis as quickly as possible. Unlike the car buying process—where we take our time, test drive multiple cars and shop for the lowest price and best financing—we want to know what's wrong with us quickly…a very different consumption motivation.

Our need for quick diagnosis (and treatment) often leads us to buy healthcare when we feel ill. 'Get me to the doctor fast' may be the mantra of someone in fear or pain. We learn that a particular specialist has an opening tomorrow. Rather than researching this specialist's qualifications, treatment specialties or experience, we take the appointment. Just imagine buying a car—or even tennis racquet—this way!

Sometimes though, we may have the time, energy and resources to research our medical consumption decisions. We may use the Web, read research reports or interview experts. Unfortunately, this likely provides little help to someone seeking a rational healthcare purchase.

Web and research information may be exhaustive and conflicting. Medical reports are often complex, requiring a degree of technical sophistication most of us lack. And reports may be biased. Who wrote the report—a pharmaceutical company, interested in selling its drugs? A surgical supply company interested in promoting its products? A research scientist interested in promoting his new procedure? A hospital interested in expanding its services? An insurance company interested in controlling costs? Absent an objective base, most consumers have difficulty using the available information to make informed healthcare purchasing decisions.

Even if consumers could understand all available literature, they need to <u>apply</u> the information to their own idiosyncratic case. This would require detailed self-diagnosis to differentiate, for example, indigestion from pancreatitis. Or to know exactly which cancer affects your lymph node. Or whether peritoneal or hemodialysis is more appropriate. Consumers typically lack sufficient medical training to self-diagnose. In addition, consumers face emotional issues in self-diagnosis—anxiety about the results may affect your diagnosis—hardly the recipe for good healthcare consumption decision making.

Yet an even larger information problem exists. When we chose a specialist for diagnosis or treatment, we want the best. After all, this is a potentially life or death decision.

Yet half (statistically) of physicians are below average. Half of hospitals too. Half of doctors graduated in the bottom half of their medical school class. Half of radiologists are below average diagnosticians; half of surgeons have below average outcomes.

Objective provider quality information only occasionally exists and—if it does exist—is very difficult to understand. Do university affiliated teaching hospitals (for example) have below average outcomes because they specialize in more difficult patients—or because they provide poorer treatment? Can an oncologist skew his outcome statistics by referring out complex cases? Can a nephrologist only accept low risk patients? Does a pediatric psychiatrist have superior abilities—or just a good bedside manner?

Since most of us make medical purchase decisions unpredictably, irregularly, idiosyncratically, quickly and potentially while ill, and since most of us cannot adequately self-diagnose or determine above average specialists, we generally seek a counselor to advise us on medical service purchasing. Our Primary Care Physician becomes our trusted advisor to guide us through this maze of medical care purchasing decisions.

The PCP provides information on which services to buy, where to buy them and how to coordinate them. We trust that our PCP knows us and the local specialists and hospitals, so will advise us appropriately. We often abdicate our own decision-making responsibilities by trusting our PCP—unlike in any other economic market. And we trust that the PCP will work in our interests.

The trust factor is particularly keen when we consider the risks of poor medical purchasing. We fear unlimited risk and must make these consumption decisions quickly. At a vulnerable time of fear, illness and uncertainty, we often <u>want</u>—as much as need—to trust our PCP.

But how can we determine if our PCP is 'good'? Remember that half of all physicians are below average. Is our physician current on the medical and pharmaceutical literature? This may be impossible with the expansion of medical knowledge and reporting, for no individual could possibly remain current on all aspects of medicine and still have time for patients. Yet we trust that our primary physician is up-to-date.

Can our PCP also keep current on the quality of local specialists? This would mean reviewing objective outcome measures of perhaps hundreds of specialists—while keeping current on the medical literature. Perhaps we trust our PCPs too much.

Indeed, evidence exists that physician referral patters follow specialist status rather than objective outcomes. Sociologist Stephen Shortell's 'Model of Physician Referral Behavior' found that physician referral patterns were heavily based on factors such as status and economics, rather than medical need and physician quality. [1] Arthur Hartz, Jose Pulido and Evelyn Kuhn found that reputations of cardiac surgeons were uncorrelated with objective ability measurements. [2] Peter Franks, et al found that PCP referral rates in Rochester, New York referred patients to specialists in patterns that could not be explained by differences in patient need. [3]

As our physician refers, presumably to the best of his or her ability, price never (depending on the patient's insurance coverage) becomes an issue. Few physicians or patients know prices for medical procedures and even fewer negotiate. Price is (practically) never a referral consideration. Imagine buying a car without regard to price!

That is exactly what Victor Fuchs and Alan Garber, two healthcare economists did in 2004 [4]:

> Imagine how the market for automobiles would have developed if a 3rd party had provided auto insurance that paid 80% (or more) of the cost of new cars…such insurance would influence both the number and types of cars people bought. People would replace cars more

often, and they would buy higher quality cars than they do in today's auto market. A Lincoln or Mercedes would cost buyers little more than a Chevrolet or a Honda, and sales of luxury automobiles would rise. Auto manufacturers would focus their product development on quality enhancements, such as big engines and luxurious interiors, rather than on cost-reducing manufacturing changes....the quality-adjusted price of autos might fall, but since only high-quality cars would be sold, the average price of a car would rise...the well-insured might welcome the steady improvements in the quality of luxury cars, but many would be better off with simpler autos and higher take-home pay.

Insurance companies take price out of the healthcare purchasing equation.

HOW THE HEALTHCARE MARKET STRUCTURE PROMOTES MORAL HAZARD

We have now set the scene to understand moral hazard's role in healthcare consumption. Individual consumers cannot make wise, informed healthcare buying decisions due to the irregularity, unpredictability and idiosyncratic nature of their purchases. Patients cannot understand the available literature, diagnose their own problems, or choose wisely among specialists and hospitals for the best—or most appropriate—treatment. As fear and time pressure force consumers to choose providers quickly, the patients abdicate their consumer sovereignty to primary care physicians—who may or may not act in the patient's interests. And since throughout this entire process the insurance carrier pays providers' bills, consumers typically don't care about price and inflation roars.

ITEM: Milton Roemer in 1961 was among the first to identify moral hazard's impact on medical consumption when he studied an upstate New York community and developed Roemer's Law: a hospital room built is a hospital room filled. In 1957 this community had 1 general hospital with 139 beds that seemed to meet community needs with an average daily census of 108—suggesting that the hospital was rarely full. In 1958, the hospital moved to a new facility with 197 beds and the occupancy rate increased to 137 (a 26% increase in 1 year)—with no change to the overall community health and no other economic factors at work. Roemer's only explanation: that physicians responded to the increased supply of beds by admitting more patients. He finds that 'the supply of hospital beds in a community or state is the major determinant of the hospital utilization rate.' (5) Physicians, interestingly, are paid fee-for-service; they only get paid when they treat.

Here is an example of our first and second types of moral hazard. Patients may have received care worth less than its cost by hospitalization in 1958 for conditions that would NOT have required hospitalization in 1957. And providers apparently take economics into consideration when designing a treatment plan: in 1958 they could hospitalize (and bill) for conditions that in 1957 were deemed unnecessary for hospitalization. (6)

ITEM: Some 20 years later, Victor Fuchs studied the 'Supply of Surgeons and Demand for Operations' (7). Fuchs learned that surgery rates are higher in regions that have more surgeons. He postulates that a 10% increase in surgeons leads to a 1—3% increase in surgeries. It seems that surgeons—who are generally paid on a fee-for-service basis—recommend more surgeries than non-surgeons do. Here is an example of our third type of moral hazard: provider tendencies to recommend the most expensive, rather than least cost medical interventions.

What impact does this element of moral hazard have on total US healthcare spending? Dr. Elliott Fisher, a Dartmouth Medical School researcher says that 'Our finding suggests that up to about a third of medical care is devoted to services that do not provide any detectable benefit'. (8) Many tests that patients demand, and hospitalizations that physicians acquiesce to add little to our healthcare outcomes but cost a great deal.

ITEM: I attempted to quantify moral hazard pharmaceutical overspending in my hometown of Easton, Massachusetts. I tried to compare prices for 10 mg of prochlorperazine (an anti-nausea medication chosen at random) at 3 pharmacies—COSTCO, CVS and Brooks. See the list prices below:

List prices for 10 mg tablets of procholoperazine, November 16, 2006

Quantity	COSTCO	CVS	Brooks
50	$10.29 ($.21/pill)	$34.29 ($.69/pill)	$30.79 ($.62/pill)
100	$14.99 ($.15/pill)	$66.99 ($.67/pill)	$51.99 ($.52/pill)

CVS and Brooks offer discounts of about 30% to AAA members who have no other pharmaceutical insurance. Even after the discount, Brooks and CVS charged over twice the COSTCO price for exactly the same medication. (9) But shoppers with Rx coverage pay the same pharmaceutical copayment at all three, typically stop price shopping at that point, and have no idea how much each insurance company pays for these drugs. Perhaps Dr. Fisher was too conservative!

ITEM: The Boston Globe noted a rise in 'Futile Care for Dying Cancer Patients' during the 1990s. (10) From a review of Medicare records the Globe reported that 12% of elderly cancer patients received chemotherapy during their last 2 weeks of life in 1999—up from 10% in 1993. The Globe also reported that 11% of these patients were admitted to Intensive Care during their last 2 weeks of life in 1999—up from 8% in 1993. (Remember—these are old and very sick patients.) The Globe claims that 'overly aggressive treatment...puts people through grueling and costly ordeals when there is no chance of a cure.' Dr. Craig Earle of Boston's Dana-Farber Cancer Institute and Harvard Medical School explains how this moral hazard arises: 'It's sometimes easier to just keep giving chemotherapy than (the alternatives).'

Here is our first type of moral hazard: providing care worth less (in terms of longevity or life quality improvements) than the treatment costs.

ITEM: Average Medicare spending on patients in Miami during their last 6 months of life was about double the Medicare spending on patients in Minneapolis during their last 6 months, according to a study by Jonathan Skinner and John Wennberg (11). Average per capita Medicare expenditures were $3,341 in Minneapolis and $8,414 in Miami. (12) Average ICU days were nearly 4 times higher in Miami. Average Miami Medicare patients had 440% more specialist visits during their last 6 months that did Medicare patients in Minneapolis.

These Medicare patients in their last 6 months of life were generally quite ill. There is no strong evidence that the spending differences were due to an underlying variation in health levels across the regions. Nor is there evidence of any benefit from higher spending levels 'The increased spending in Miami does not translate to improved life expectancy' say the authors.

In Minneapolis, home health services are 39% of the national average, while in Miami they are 60% above average, meaning their ratio is roughly 4 to 1. By contrast, the inpatient service ratio is only 1.5 to 1, suggesting that services with the greatest discretionary (and profitability) component—home health and laboratory services—are the ones most sensitive to geographic location.

'There appears to be little correlation between the intensity of care near the end of life and mortality rates, whether intensity is measured by spending, days in the hospital, or ICU days near the end of life,' according to the study.

What explains these cost differences? After all, Medicare is a federal program with national standards and provider reimbursement rates, modified slightly for cost of living variations geographically. The authors suggest that

> 'one reason could be the sheer amount of resources in Miami, more hospital beds per thousand [Roemer's Law??] and more specialists (46% more in Miami). Another explanation could be the much higher ratio of for-profit hospital beds in Miami, 56 percent versus 2 percent in Minneapolis...(still another) could in the structure of physician groups rather than hospitals. The interaction between patient demand and physician behavior is also important in understanding the practice of medicine in Miami...elderly patients come to expect numerous referrals as the norm, and would suspect physicians who do not refer them to other physicians.'

Wennberg gives an interesting explanation of this process. (13) First, there is no clear rulebook for dealing with chronically ill patients. When should an elderly cancer patient who also suffers from congestive heart disease be admitted to hospital either for treatment or observation? How ill must a patient be for a physician to prescribe home health care? How often should a patient suffering from congestive heart failure be seen by a cardiologist—every 2 months? Every 3 months? Every 4 months?

Wennberg suggests that the physician 'will sort it out based on how sick an individual patient is and <u>how many openings he has in his schedule.</u> Specialists tend to fill their appointment books to capacity' (emphasis my own) making it easy to see how increasing the supply of cardiologists would mean patients will see their physicians more often.

But patients are also complicit in this Medicare extravaganza claims Gina Kolata in the New York Times. (14) Doctor visits

> 'have become a social activity…Many patients have 8, 10 or 12 specialists and visit one or more of them most days of the week. They bring their spouses and plan their days around their appointments, going out to eat or shopping while they are in the area. They know what they want; they choose specialists for every body part. And every visit, every procedure is covered by Medicare…Boca Raton, researchers agree, is a case study of what happens when people are given free rein to have all the medical care they could imagine.'

How do patients find appropriate specialists? Leon Bloomberg, age 83 tells us: 'You get recommendations at the clubhouse, at the swimming pool. You go to a restaurant here and 9 out of 10 times, before the meal is over, you hear people talking about a doctor.' Apparently Miami residents think clubhouse friends and swimming pool companions have equal diagnostic and referral credibility to technically trained physicians.

Providers claim excessive patient demand—patients want lots of tests and specialists, they refer themselves to specialists and they ask for and get far more medical attention than many doctors think is reasonable or advisable. The Medicare card is 'like a gold card that lets you go to any doctor you want' claims Dr. Robert Colton, a Boca Raton internist. 'I see it every day.'

But Dr. Colton sounds a cautionary note, worrying that Primary Care Physicians cannot perform their gate-keeping function properly. 'When there's no control on utilization, (physicians take) the path of least resistance. If a patient says 'My shoulder hurts, I want an M.R.I., I want to see a shoulder specialist,' the path of least resistance is to send them off. You have nothing to gain by refusing.'

Specialists can take advantage of this situation by providing (fee-for-service) tests and procedures with high Medicare reimbursements. A nuclear stress test for example pays the doctor about $200 and the medical facility about $1200. 'Doctors have incorporated these tests…into their offices so they can gain from the facility fee' says Dr. Thomas Bartzokis, a cardiologist in Boca Raton.

'The doctors are raping Medicare' claims Louis Ziegler, a retired manufacturer living in nearby Delray Beach. He recalled a doctor's visit for a chronic finger problem and requested a cortisone shot. But he got much more. 'I had diathermy. I had ultrasound. I had a paraffin massage. I had $600 worth of Medicare treatments to get my lousy $35 shot of cortisone.'

In other words, moral hazard rules in Miami. Patients demand service, providers bill and Medicare pays—about double per capita compared to Minneapolis for approximately the same epidemiological population, with no obvious longevity or life quality improvements. Miami Medicare subscribers self-diagnose and self-refer, apparently at whim. Everyone, it seems, takes advantage of the fact that 'Medicare pays.' And our Miami friends receive lots of care where benefits are worth less than costs.

ITEM: Viagra sales soar even though exercise produces better results. Pfizer sells $1.7 billion of Viagra annually to fight erectile dysfunction. Many insurance carriers cover a monthly dosage. Pfizer advertises heavily to stimulate demand for this product.

But simple exercise produces better results, according to a Harvard Magazine report on a study comparing the effects of exercise to sildenafil, the active ingredient in Viagra. Men with erectile dysfunction and mild to moderate circulation problems engaged in a program of squatting exercise and pelvic and leg lifts designed to improve blood flow to the pelvis, buttocks and upper leg muscles. After two years, 80% of the exercisers reported better erections, compared with only 74% taking sildenafil. (15)

Studies such as these are not well known, for no large companies promote the (virtually cost free) exercise program that could save consumers hundreds of millions of dollars annually—and produce better results! Instead, companies seeking to solve erectile dysfunction problems design products for which they can bill carriers, and advertise heavily to attract consumers. No one markets other, potentially cheaper and more effective treatments. After all...why segment the market when the insurance company pays for the expensive treatments?

This Viagra example shows our third definition of moral hazard—provider recommendation of an expensive, rather than low cost intervention—to serve their interests.

ITEM: Short-term survival interventions among the elderly vary up to 674 percent by region. Skinner, et al find a great divergence by US geographic region in specific medical procedures that are used to maintain survival among seriously and chronically ill patients. These include insertions of emergency airways, dialysis for failing kidneys, feeding tubes inserted into the stomach, and mechanical breathing assistance. These, according to the authors are 'not designed to improve quality of life but instead are directed toward maintaining short-term survival'. (16) The authors compare rates of specific procedures per 1000 decedents by regional frequency of physician visits in the last six months of life:

Intervention	Region in the highest decile of MD visits during last 6 months of life	Region in the lowest decile of MD visits during last 6 months of life	Ratio
Insertion of Emergency Airways	140	42	3.33
Hemodialysis (for kidney failure)	384	87	4.41
Gastrostomy Tube Placement (feeding tube)	136	25	5.44
Continuous Ventilator Mgt (mechanical breathing apparatus)	387	50	7.74

These procedures are short-term fixes at best for a population with 6 or fewer months to live.

The authors suggest that Medicare spends nearly 20% of its budget ($26 billion in 1996) on procedures like these that appear to provide no benefit in terms of longevity or increased quality of life. Indeed, they

'find little evidence that the greater spending observed in the high-intensity regions leads to better health outcomes...on the other hand, regional indicators of effective practice—rates of screening for breast cancer, influenza vaccinations, and appropriate treatment of heart attacks—are associated strongly with improved survival. In short...the Medicare program provides too little in the way of inexpensive and effective care, while at the same time spending $26 billion annually or 20% of it's budget for health care of questionable value' (page 4)

But providers can bill Medicare for emergency dialysis or tube insertions. As Dr. Earle of Boston's Dana-Farber Hospital reminds us, it's sometimes easier to keep giving care than the alternative. It's certainly more profitable.

Interestingly, private employer-based health insurance payments also seem tied to geographic regions. The Dartmouth Atlas of Health Care in Michigan (17) reports similar spending patterns for Blue Cross and Blue Shield. When patients demand more care and providers acquiesce, spending soars—whether taxpayers or private carriers pay the bills. Moral hazard knows no differentiation.

Here we see examples of all three of our moral hazard definitions: (1) treatment plans where costs exceed benefits, (2) treatment plans that include economic considerations, and (3) provision of higher cost, rather than lower cost options.

ITEM: Lubbock, Texas has become the heart-care industry's El Dorado. The Wall Street Journal reports (18) that in 1995 Texas doctors did angiograms on 45% of Medicare patients following heart attacks, while New York doctors did them in only 30% of cases. The greater Texas frequency did not, on the whole, save lives or improve patients' well-being, says Edward Guadagnoli, a Harvard Medical School professor who led the study.

But the greater frequency did allow Texas cardiologists to bill Medicare $8,000 or more per procedure. Angioplasty became so lucrative in the late 1980s that some Lubbock cardiologists leased helicopters to bring emergency cases in from outlying rural areas. Since, however, many of these areas lacked helipads, the cardiologists had to build them. 'We hired contractors to pour concrete in at least 20 towns,' said Dr. Howard Hurd of Cardiology Associates.

In most of the US, tiny rural hospitals treat heart-attack patients on site, giving clot-busting drugs. But Lubbock cardiologists told rural physicians that patients needed to be flown to their cath lab for emergency angiograms and angioplasties. Result: a $3,000 helicopter bill per case, a $2,000 cardiologist fee and a $12,000 Lubbock hospital bill. The doctors designed their treatments around insurance company reimbursement policies.

Cardiologist Dr. Robert Wey, a partner in Lubbock's Cardiology Associates, described this situation saying 'I thought I'd died and gone to heaven.' In 1995, 11 of the group's 14 doctors earned more than $1 million—figures that astound cardiologists elsewhere. Nationally, invasive cardiologists earned an average of about $350,000. (19)

But who's to complain? Tim Weitz, chief counsel at the Texas State Board of Medical Examiners explains that claims of unnecessary angioplasty 'are very difficult to prove. Maybe 9 out of 10 doctors will disagree with what the physician did. Maybe with hindsight he shouldn't have done the procedure.' But if doctors can produce expert witnesses justifying a procedure, regulators will be hard-pressed to prevail in a disciplinary case.

And Cardiology Associates provided one of the few economic growth forces in Lubbock, eliminating most local economic incentives to reduce the medical gravy train.

Who really loses by all this apparent excess of medical treatment? Certainly not the local economy. Nor the local hospitals or their employees. Nor most patients who receive high technology care—even if it's more care than necessary and sometimes the risks exceed the benefits. As long as the insurance company (or Medicare) pays, then everyone benefits and moral hazard continues to consume tremendous medical resources.

Cardiology Associates practice our second and third types of moral hazard: treatment plans that include economic considerations (ie carrier reimbursement policies) and provision of more expensive, rather than less expensive medical interventions based on provider preference.

Where does this all end? With consumers demanding medical treatment (without regard to cost), and providers willing to acquiesce, can we see a final endpoint where the healthcare marketplace creates a monument to moral hazard?

Perhaps we do in Indianapolis. In 2002, the average Indianapolis insurance reimbursement for coronary by-pass surgery was $29,300, with an average net profit of $6,800, or 23%—quite good for any business. (20) In 2002—to take advantage of these good margins—the Heart Center of Indiana opened a new 60 bed cardiac unit. This began a Medical Arms Race. Between 2002—2004, Indianapolis' 4 other major hospitals invested $220 million to renovate, expand and add 20% new cardiac surgical capacity, making a total of 5 open heart surgery programs for

1.6 million people. Unfortunately, there was no evidence of need: open-heart volumes had been falling for 2 years from 4,377 procedures in 2002 to 3,310 in 2004 as patients opted for less invasive procedures. Not to worry suggested Tom Malasto, Executive Director of the Cardiac and Vascular Care Center at St. Francis Hospital in 2004. 'The most recent CDC statistics place Indiana as one of the top five states for obesity and prevalence of smoking'.

The Indianapolis facilities chose to wait for—or induce—demand for expensive heart surgeries. Rather than invest in obesity prevention, low cost treatments or smoking secession programs, huge investments went into expensive surgical facilities. Had this been normal economic competition, we would expect the various producers to segment their market—one supplier aiming at expensive procedures, another at low-cost alternatives—and then advertising for customers. Or, if all suppliers aimed at the expensive market segment, we would expect prices to fall.

But prices don't fall when hospitals compete. No surgeon wants to operate in a second-rate facility and no patient wants second-rate care. Once the Heart Center of Indiana opened it's new 60-bed facility in 2002 all the other hospitals had to follow. They needed to keep their cardiac surgeons happy or feared losing them to the new Heart Center. Jack Finn, director of the New Orleans Metropolitan Hospital Council summarized this problem: 'When you get hospital competition in a city it drives costs up, not down. The competition is for doctors, not patients. And if you're going to compete for doctors, you have to have state-of-the-art equipment' (21)

But the biggest problem has yet to arise.

Medical researchers have known for years about the volume-outcome relationship in medicine. Hospitals and surgeons having the most experience with specific procedures have the lowest mortality rates, and those with the least experience have the highest mortality rates. This stands to reason as 'practice makes perfect'. Indeed the Leapfrog Group, a respected medical industry think-thank that monitors hospital quality, recommends a 450 coronary bypass surgery annual hospital minimum; below that, the mortality rates increase.

If the number of heart surgeries in Indianapolis continues to drop by 533/year for 2 more years (as it had from 2002—2004), then by 2007 all 5 cardiac facilities will average only 448 by-pass surgeries annually—below the recommended safety volume!

Indianapolis shows the macro-economic extension of moral hazard—the Medical Arms Race. Unfortunately, this race is on going in virtually every American city, for many types of medical treatment.

WHY THIS IS IMPORTANT

Some economists believe that our society should treat healthcare like all other forms of economic activity and let the marketplace alone decide which suppliers prosper and which fail. These economists think that the normal market mechanism of consumers registering their demand for various healthcare products with their 'dollar votes', and suppliers offering a wide variety of (unregulated) products and services will promote an efficient healthcare system.

In the words of John Goodman, Gerald Musgrave and Devon Herrick, our core healthcare problem is that governmental regulations 'have suppressed the ability of the market to allocate health care resources' (22), and that we should treat the healthcare market like we treat the market for automobiles or wine. A less regulated market would be more efficient and equitable they say. Proponents of this approach support a reduction in governmental healthcare regulations.

Others believe that the differences between the healthcare market and all other economic markets are so great as to require more governmental regulation and intervention. These people often support single payer, highly governmentally regulated health systems. To quote Drs. Julius Richmond (former US Surgeon General and Professor Emeritus at Harvard University), and Rashi Fein (Professor Emeritus of Medical Economics at Harvard University),

> 'We believe that the most effective, efficient, and equitable health care insurance system would be…single payer…its financing would rely on tax revenues…(it) would enable us to attain…universal coverage…social cohesion and progressivity' (23)

Various surveys have shown that a majority of Americans support the single payer philosophy. We will evaluate single payer systems in Chapter 5 and help the reader evaluate public policy implications of these two polar opposite positions.

CONCLUSION

We began this analysis by considering the differences between car buying and medical service buying. We have seen that individuals cannot make informed healthcare consumption decisions without help from their trusted primary care physician. We have also seen that PCPs refer to specialists and hospitals based as much on reputation and economics as on medical outcomes. And we have seen how hospitals compete for physicians in a medical arms race that drives up costs with no obvious or direct relationship to outcomes.

Let's turn in the next chapter to ways that moral hazard infects indemnity based health insurance—the most common form of US health insurance until about 1990.

Chapter 1: Notes

1. S. Shortell, 'A Model of Physician Referral Behavior: A Test of Exchange Theory in Medical Practice', University of Chicago Center for Health Administration Studies Research Series Number 31. This and the next 3 notes come from David Dranove, 'The Economic Evolution of American Healthcare', Princeton University Press, 2000, page 41. I used many of Dranove's concepts and ideas in the first half of this Chapter.

2. J. Pulido, A Hartz, and E. Kuhn, 'Are the Best Coronary Artery Bypass Surgeons Identified by Physician Surveys?' American Journal of Public Health 87 (1997): 1645-48

3. P. Franks, et al., 'Variations in Primary Care Physicians, Referral Rates,' Health Services Research 34, Number 1 (1999): 323-29

4. Quoted in Henry Aaron, et al 'Can We Say No' Brookings Institution Press, 2005, page 2

5. Milton Roemer, 'Bed Supply and Hospital Utilization: A Natural Experiment', Hospitals, 35 (1961), page 36

6. There is an alternative explanation. In 1957 and earlier, physicians could have been providing inferior care—a situation that the 1958 hospital expansion cured. This seems statistically unlikely, however, as the 1957 hospital bed utilization rate averaged only about 78%.

7. Victor Fuchs 'Supply of Surgeons and Demand for Operations' Journal of Human Resources 13 (1978):35-56, discussed in Dranove, 'Economic Evolution of American Healthcare', page 34

8. Elliott S. Fisher, 'HealthCare in America: Is More Better?' Annals of Internal Medicine, February 2003, quoted in Maggie Mahar, 'Money Driven Healthcare', page 28. Fisher and colleagues compared regional Medicare spending difference and health outcomes. They found that, while Medicare recipients living in high spending areas had more physician visits, more tests and more hospitalizations, they showed no evidence of lower death rates or better health status.

9. Though COSTCO is normally a membership club, the pharmacy does not require COSTCO membership.

10. Boston Globe, June 3, 2006, page 3 'Futile Care for Dying Cancer Patients on Rise'

11. Jonathan Skinner, John E. Wennberg 'How Much is Enough? Efficiency and Medicare Spending in the Last Six Months of Life' NBER Working Paper 6513, 1998. All quotes in this ITEM come from this paper.

12. These are 1996 Medicare expenditure data discussed in Wennberg and Cooper 'The Quality of Medical Care in the United States: A Report on the Medicare Program' The Dartmouth Atlas of Health Care in the United States. American Health Association Press, Chicago, 1999

13. Wennberg's analysis comes from Mahar 'Money-Driven Medicine' page 172

14. Gina Kolata 'Patients in Florida Lining Up for All That Medicare Covers' New York Times, September 13, 2003 page A1. All quotes from this article.

15. Jonathan Shaw, 'The Deadliest Sin' Harvard Magazine, March-April 2004, pages 36—99. This information is on page 39

16. 'The Efficiency of Medicare', Jonathan Skinner, Elliott S. Fisher and John E. Wennberg, Working Paper 8395, National Bureau of Economic Research, July, 2001, page 13.

17. J.E.Wennberg and D.E.Wennberg, eds 'The Dartmouth Atlas of Health Care in Michigan' (Hanover, New Hampshire:

Center for the Evaluative Clinical Sciences, Dartmouth Medical School, 2000), reported in Mahar 'Money Driven Healthcare', page 160

18. 'Maximum Medicine: In Lubbock, Texas, A Weak Heart Gets the Full Treatment' George Anders, The Wall Street Journal, July 16, 1996, page A1. All quotes and references come from this article.

19. See Edward Martin 'Physician Pay Remains Stagnant' American College of Physicians, CEP-ASIM Observer, November 1998. Martin reports that in 1997 invasive cardiologists' incomes averaged $326,537, down 7.7% from 1996.

20. This Indianapolis example comes from Mahar, 'Money-Driven Medicine' pp 40—41.

21. New Orleans Times Picayune, Oct 16, 1984—reported in Mahar, 'Money Driven Healthcare'.

22. John C. Goodman, Gerald L. Musgrave and Devon M. Herrick, 'Lives at Risk', Rowman & Littlefield Publishers, Inc, 2004, page 7

23. Julius B. Richmond and Rashi Fein, 'The Health Care Mess' Harvard University Press, 2005, pp 243-244. Emphasis added.

CHAPTER 2
Moral Hazard in Indemnity Health Insurance

The US health insurance system originated in Dallas, Texas in 1929.

Early in the Great Depression, Baylor University Hospital suffered a cash flow problem: the high unemployment rate resulted in few patients able to pay for treatment. The Hospital had traditionally relied on a combination of charitable donations and paying customers to balance its books. But as unemployment grew, the rate of paying customers decreased.

The Hospital's dilemma: how to increase the rate of paying customers during a period of growing unemployment. Very cleverly, the Hospital turned to Dallas' largest employer—the Dallas school system—for the solution.

Baylor University Hospital offered to provide hospital services to any Dallas teacher in return for a bi-weekly payment of $.50 from each teacher. The bi-weekly payments stabilized hospital cash flow and the treatment guarantee enticed the teachers to pay. This arrangement reduced risk to both parties—the hospital would stay in business and teachers would avoid potential financial ruin for hospital care.

THE CONCEPTUAL EVOLUTION OF INDEMNITY HEALTH INSURANCE

Note the key components of Baylor's plan. The hospital **marketed** to a large employer group. This benefited the hospital by reducing sales and marketing expenses. Our long national relationship between health insurance and employer groups began with Baylor University Hospital in Dallas and continues to this day.

Baylor University Hospital, second, provided **sickness treatment** but no preventive medicine. Remember the reason that Baylor established this program: to guarantee payment from hospital patients. At that time hospitals were not in the 'preventive medicine' business, nor was this plan designed to keep people healthy.

And third, the Hospital acted as both **insurance carrier and provider**. Baylor Hospital paid physicians on salary—not fee-for-service—and thus eliminated a potential moral hazard risk. Physicians had no financial incentive to order superfluous tests or procedures. Indeed, physicians might have the opposite incentive, to undertreat (as a cost-control measure) in hope of receiving a bonus or promotion.

These three elements—employer marketing, sickness treatment and linked funding source and provider—are at the core of future American health insurance. Once the Baylor model proved successful, other hospitals and cities copied it to avoid being left out of an important financial trend. This financing arrangement benefited the hospitals, especially as depression-era unemployment rates remained high.

However—as is typical in a competitive, capitalistic economy—healthcare purchasers soon demanded additional services including choice among hospitals. This fundamentally altered Baylor's model. With patients able to chose among several independent hospitals, no longer could each function as financier <u>and</u> provider. A new entity was required to handle financing alone and leave hospitals to their traditional provider role.

The revenue collecting entities became independent insurance carriers (Blue Cross was the largest) and hospitals (generally) limited themselves to billing for services rendered.

This split between financier (insurance carrier) and provider opened the door to moral hazard and the medical arms race. Each hospital wanted to increase billings by providing more patient services. Each hospital also wanted to attract the best physicians (and their patients) by offering the latest medical equipment and finest operating theatres. Once the finance and provider functions split, hospitals developed their own set of financial interests that were often in conflict with the carriers' interests.

Physicians also wanted to share in this lucrative carrier-billing business, as the Depression Era unemployment rates also limited their fee-collections and revenue streams. Blue Shield developed to finance physician services, much as Blue Cross financed hospital services.

By the mid-1930s, the basic US indemnity health insurance formula was established. Health insurance was sold at the workplace, via employers. Carriers established policies and prices. Providers—hospitals and physicians—billed the carriers (or subscribers who received carrier reimbursement) for services rendered. As insurance developed over the next 75 years, these three groups remained the key players.

INDEMNITY PLAN FORM AND FUNCTION

Insurers indemnify subscribers for medical treatment after-the-fact. The subscriber receives treatment, pays the provider, and then submits the bill to the carrier for indemnification. Carriers indemnify the subscriber according to coverage provisions. Typically indemnification plans include a deductible and a co-insurance rate. For example, the subscriber might have an annual deductible of, say $500 and 80% co-insurance—means the carrier pays 80% of all allowed costs above the deductible.

Carriers often pay 'standard and customary' fees to providers, according to the carriers' fee schedule. For example, a carrier might typically pay $500 for setting a broken forearm or $3500 for removing a gall bladder. If the provider charges more, the subscriber pays the difference.

Or the carrier might indemnify the subscriber based on 'cost-plus reimbursement'. The carrier might pay the provider for actual medical treatment costs, provided the costs seem reasonable—plus an overhead factor.

Indemnity health insurance plans only pay for medical services provided, creating a potentially powerful financial incentive for physicians and hospitals to perform tests and procedures. Indemnity plans typically pay very little (or nothing) for <u>preventing</u> medical treatments. With cost-plus reimbursement, providers have little financial incentive to offer low cost treatments and a significant financial incentive to perform the most expensive available procedures. At the same time, indemnity carriers typically allow physicians and hospitals wide latitude to use their best judgements when designing medical treatments.

Economically, indemnity carriers' primary concerns are continued financial strength (i.e., maintaining appropriate payout percentages) and policy sales. The carrier can maintain appropriate payout percentages by correctly pricing policies—a fairly complex underwriting/actuarial task based largely on history and experience. When considering payout rates, the carrier doesn't particularly care what the actual policies <u>cost</u>—only that prices remain in line with payout.

Policy costs becomes relevant when the carrier wants to renew existing plans or expand its market share. Experience shows that price is but one factor that consumers consider when renewing. Other—often more important factors—include the range of coverage, customer service and size of provider network...and may explain some of the carriers apparent lack of interest in controlling physician and hospital treatments.

Studies suggest (1) that access to treatment and lack of carrier interference can rate as highly—or even more highly—in subscriber renewal calculations than price. Remember how trust plays a key role in medical purchasing—how a patient's trust in the physician can overwhelm all other factors when buying medical treatment. Insurance carriers have apparently learned that they can maintain high renewal rates by supporting these trusted PCPs and specialists, rather than by attempting to control them.

MORAL HAZARD ENTERS THE PICTURE

David Dranove, in The Economic Evolution of American Health Care, suggests three reasonable types of provider induced moral hazards. (2)

First, provider induced moral hazard arises due to vague or confusing diagnoses, which allow the physician to try various tests, procedures and treatments before deciding which serves the patient best.

Second, given such clinical ambiguity, physicians reimbursed on fee-for-service schedules, or hospitals with cost-plus reimbursement might recommend the most costly interventions.

Third, hospital administrators may be under pressure to keep beds full and therefore not object to treatment inefficiencies. (3)

Two studies in the 1970s—at the height of indemnity coverage's market share in the US—shed some on the magnitude of moral hazard under indemnity health insurance. Anne Scitovsky and Melda McCall (4) studied health service consumption among Stanford University employees, both before and after imposition of a 25% copayment for physician services. Scitovsky and McCall found that the copayment imposition decreased the number of physician visits by 24% with no apparent change to the health status of Stanford employees.

The RAND Corporation studied healthcare consumption patterns by over 6,000 people with the same indemnity health coverage but different levels of copayments. (5) One set of people had no copayments; others ranged from 25—95% of the medical bill, up to $1000 per individual. This multi-year study also compared before and after health status data. RAND concluded that people receiving free care generated about 30% more medical bills than people facing copayments. However, even after 5 years of study people in the high medical consumption group were not measurably healthier.

Interestingly, the RAND 1970s determination of a 30% waste factor coincides with Dr. Fisher's 2003 estimate discussed in Chapter 1.

The opportunities for moral hazard offered by indemnity health insurance led to a tremendous increase in healthcare spending during the 1960s, 70s and 80s. Total US healthcare spending increased from $27 billion in 1960 to $73 billion in 1970, to $257 billion by 1980 and to $700 billion by 1990. This represented a growth from 5.2% of US GDP going to healthcare in 1960 to 12.6% in 1990.

Some of this increase resulted from introducing Medicaid and Medicare in the 1960s. These two programs aimed at providing health insurance to people without access to employer based coverage—the poor and elderly. Both programs grew rapidly, with total Medicaid and Medicare spending growing from about $8 billion in 1967 to about $27 billion in 1976. Spending grew faster than the supply of doctors and hospitals. One effect of these programs (there were many others) was healthcare inflation: many new patients and much more money chased (basically) the same number of providers. A fairly classic inflation scenario—increased demand with a constrained supply.

The government worried about need to raise taxes if entitlement programs continued to grow so quickly. And the health insurance industry began to consider cost control (read 'moral hazard control') options.

HOSPITAL COST CONTROL PROGRAMS

New York State that had the largest Medicaid program, developed the first **rate setting program** in 1970. The New York legislature proposed to cap Medicaid hospital payments and included private carriers in the program to avoid hospital cost shifting.

The New York State Prospective Rate Setting System established a flat fee per patient per day. The fee was set at the beginning of each year so hospitals could budget and plan, and was approximately equal to the average cost per patient per day the previous year with an inflation factor and regional cost variations applied.

This rather blunt system changed the hospital reimbursement paradigm by putting hospitals at financial risk. No longer would New York allow blind cost-plus reimbursement to enrich providers while potentially bankrupting the state. Rather, the state wanted to control hospital expenditures to keep entitlement benefits attractive and taxes under control.

There is some evidence that this prospective rate setting program achieved intended results. Dranove compared inflation rates under prospective payment systems with rates under traditional cost-plus reimbursement and discovered about 1.5% lower inflation under PRS. (6)

This was apparently enough to start a trend. New Jersey introduced its Medicare Prospective Rate Setting System—quite different from New York's—in the late 1970s. New Jersey modified New York's calculation of average cost/patient/day by introducing 470 **Diagnosis Related Groups** (DRGs). This system, designed by Yale Medical School, divided patient costs into diagnostic groups. Cancer surgery received a higher reimbursement than a simple overnight observation; brain surgery a higher fee than a TURP (a common prostate treatment).

This seemed to satisfy all parties. Hospitals would receive appropriate payment for medical treatment, but no more; patients would receive necessary care, but no more; and medical cost inflation would be controlled. There would be little opportunity for moral hazard as all tests and treatments would be codified by DRG.

Medicare took the New Jersey system national in the mid-1980s. Initial evidence indicated success. From 1983—1985—from just before to just after national adoption—the annual number of Medicare hospital stays declined by 4%. The average hospital stay declined by 10%, from 10.3 to 9.3 days. And annual hospital cost inflation fell from 13% to 8%. (7)

How did hospitals control their costs? Many shifted to more outpatient surgeries—not necessarily a bad thing. In 1984 some 28% of all community hospital surgeries were outpatient; by 1996 that percentage had increased to 59%.

Others simply managed their DRGs. Some hospitals hired DRG experts to help 'up-classify' patients to receive higher reimbursements. Others began 'dumping' expensive patients who exceeded their DRG reimbursements, by transferring them to other hospitals—presumably with less sophisticated admissions procedures. Some hospitals practiced 'skimming', by admitting only potentially profitable patients. Still others engaged in 'unbundling' services, or requiring patients to make more hospital visits at higher reimbursements, often with no additional health benefits.

The DRG effort helped control Medicare inpatient spending between 1985—1997 to about 8% annually. This compares to all other Medicare spending which grew at about 12% annually (suggesting that savvy hospitals shifted costs) for an average Medicare spending increase during these 12 years of about 9.5%. In other words, Medicare costs/member/year rose 3% faster than US GDP/person. (8) During this period, private sector spending increased by about 7.3% annually.

Perhaps the biggest effect of DRG imposition was a change in hospital culture. Hospitals previously were generally non-profits, funded by charitable contributions and cost-plus reimbursement, facing little financial risk. As Dranove says

> Until the early 1980s, the managers of nonprofit health care organizations were under little financial pressure. Market conditions enabled even badly managed hospitals to survive. Private insurers either paid whatever price the hospital charged or paid the hospital for its costs plus a predetermined profit margin...(hospitals) that provided unprofitable services or cared for the uninsured covered the expenses by charging higher prices to everyone else. (9)

Physicians had traditionally run hospitals, leaving administrators to manage bookkeeping, purchasing and other defined line functions.

DRGs changed this. By putting hospitals at financial risk, DRGs required hospital investment in sophisticated accounting and business management. Hospitals now had to allocate overhead—how much depreciation to allocate by DRG for a patient presenting with multiple symptoms?—to satisfy Medicare auditors and remain in business. No easy feat.

DRGs unintentionally opened a Pandora's box of potential moral hazard opportunities to hospitals. Once hospitals began hiring sophisticated MBAs and giving them true management responsibility, DRG management became a profession. MBAs learned how to manage hospitals...and then began buying them.

Once they learned the hospital administration business, MBAs saw three particularly attractive reasons to own hospitals. First, hospitals had good, long term cash flow provided by the government and private carriers. Second, implementing sound business practices could control hospital expenses—something insufficiently widespread in non-profit hospitals. And third, hospitals could design sophisticated accounting and billing systems to increase profits.

So attractive were these opportunities that investor-owned systems acquired over 100 hospitals by 1975; 273 hospitals by 1980 and nearly 500 hospitals (plus 200 more under management contract) by 1985. (10) Today investor-owned hospital networks dominate the landscape, and companies such as Partners Community Health Plan in Boston and the Sutter system in California 'are unabashed about flaunting their power, publicly stating their intention to use their leverage when negotiating rates with managed care purchasers.' (11)

In other words, moral hazard had beaten DRGs.

Economists could have predicted this. Hospitals require insurance carrier and Medicaid/Medicare cash flow to survive. When DRGs threatened that survival, hospitals fought back. Hospitals improved their management, learned the DRG game (as so often in capitalist economics, knowledge is power) and manipulated the system to their own advantage.

Why hadn't hospitals improved their management prior to DRG implementation? And why hadn't investor groups purchased hospitals in large numbers prior to this? While we cannot recreate the mindsets of hospital administrators or investors in the early 1970s, I propose the following hypothesis: that there was no perceived need for change. The traditional system of non-profit community hospitals seemed to work fine for most interested parties. Hospitals stayed in business, physicians got paid, patients trusted their doctors, insurance carriers remained profitable and moral hazard ran amok. The AMA—the voice of America's medical community—strongly supported the traditional system. No organized opposition group had sufficient strength to change all this.

Certainly people tried. President Truman pushed for National Health Insurance in the early 1950s; Nixon passed the HMO Act of 1973 with some limited short term effects (see next chapter); Jimmy Carter tried for National Health Insurance in the 1970s. The business community wanted change, as evidenced by Fortune Magazine's editorial in January, 1970 that

> Much of US medical care, particularly the everyday business of preventing and treating routine illnesses, is inferior in quality, wastefully dispenses, and inequitably financed...most Americans are badly served by the obsolete, overstrained medical system that has grown up around them helter-skelter...The time has come for radical change...the management of medical care has become too important to leave to doctors, who, after all, are not managers to begin with.

But the existing system of non-profit hospitals and cost-plus reimbursement worked well for enough groups—hospitals, doctors and insurance carriers—that they protected it against frontal attacks by the government or business community.

Now DRGs posed a threat that upset the traditional comfortable system. Not a political threat or frontal attack—no Senate debates, marketing campaigns or huge political lobbying—but a subtle threat. DRGs were an accounting change, a detail that put hospitals' cash flow at risk.

And hospitals had to respond, think 'outside-the-box' and fight back to retain their position. This subtle accounting change altered the mindset of hospital administrators and investors, and began our national shift to investor-owned and professionally managed hospitals. Hospitals felt they <u>had</u> to maintain control over their billing function. Though regulators won some DRG battles, within 25 years hospitals won the DRG war. Moral hazard would continue.

HOSPITAL QUALITY CONTROL PROGRAMS

As Diagnosis Related Groups were aimed at controlling hospital costs, so various measures were introduced in the 1970s to control hospital quality. These aimed primarily at ensuring that patients received appropriate hospitalization and care. But they also aimed to control the moral hazard of excessive or unnecessary tests and treatment.

They fared no better than DRGs.

The first Professional Standard Review Organizations (PSROs) began in 1972. These were established by the Social Security Amendments of 1972 to 'promote the effective, efficient, and economical delivery of health care services of proper quality for which payments may be made.' (12) PSROs were local physician organizations designed to monitor the necessity, appropriateness and quality of hospital care, primarily for Medicare and Medicaid. PSROs established standards of care for a wide range of diseases, with a goal of treatment practice uniformity.

These organizations were quite ineffective. The Congressional Budget Office concluded in 1979 that PSROs reduced hospital utilization by about 2%. The CBO also concluded (based on data provided by the Health Care Finance Administration) that net savings from the PSRO program amounted to less than one-tenth of 1 percent of the relevant Medicare expenditures. (13).

Why was this? Dranove suggests that local physicians were generally reluctant to punish their colleagues. PSROs created dilemmas for physicians who observed poor quality or excessive treatment in others. Should they report on physicians who unnecessarily bring patients into the hospital and increase everyone's income? Should they be team players? Or should they fight other physicians and hospital administrators and create problems for themselves? Most physicians decided their interests— financial and professional—lay in getting along with their colleagues rather than reporting on them.

Regulators grasped this problem and modified the PSRO concept when creating the next quality control mechanism, the Professional Review Organization (PRO) in 1983. These were private companies, initially contracted by Medicaid. PROs were designed to assure the necessity and appropriateness of Medicaid services by reviewing hospital records for evidence of upcoding, dumping or unbundling of services. PROs established elaborate guidelines and enforcement protocols, again focusing on physicians and hospitals working in a particular locale.

Unfortunately, the process of developing guidelines introduced an even bigger problem—startling variations in medical practice across seemingly similar communities. (14) A famous early study 'Are Hospital Services Rationed in New Haven or Over-Utilized in Boston' (15) reported that rates of certain procedures including coronary artery bypass graft surgery rates were much higher in New Haven than Boston, but rates of other procedures such as carotid endarterectomy were higher in Boston than New Haven.

Studies such as this (16) suggested the PRO focus was too narrow and that the real hospital quality problem involved treatment variations. These not only put patients at risk but also drove up costs, for some patients were <u>over-treated</u>. Charles Phelps estimated that the total national cost of variation in coronary artery bypass graft treatment alone approached $1 billion. (17).

Such data spurred development of Treatment Guidelines, with a goal of standardizing medical treatments to control both costs and quality. Treatment guidelines typically provide the medical staff with detailed day-by-day instructions for testing, nursing, surgery, rehabilitation and discharge planning. Guidelines also provide a systemized method of ordering tests.

Unfortunately, contradictory treatment guidelines proliferated. By 1994 the AMA reported over 1600 sets of guidelines designed by (potentially) competing special interests. Hospital guidelines said 'treat' but carrier guidelines said 'don't treat'. Some guidelines were developed by pharmaceuticals and recommended drug therapy; others by surgical supply manufacturers and recommended surgery. Hospital bureaucracies and physicians resisted the imposition of guidelines, which ultimately became voluntary and only marginally effective.

Regulators next turned to Utilization Review to overcome the narrow focus of PROs and ambiguity of Treatment Guidelines.

Utilization Review is a screening procedure to determine (a) if the patient should be admitted, (b) surgical second opinions and (c) on-going review of high cost cases. Supporters claim that this ensures appropriate treatment and reduces variation and cost, while detractors claim unnecessary interference in the physician-patient relationship. There is no objective, conclusive evidence either way.

Independent 'objective' companies perform Utilization Review. These companies have developed best practice criteria. Through evaluation of outcome measures, UR companies have developed illness-specific screens. Procedurally, the hospital admissions nurse reports clinical data and a treatment plan to a UR nurse, who runs the information through the screens. The UR nurse may agree to hospitalization, recommend outpatient treatment or even refuse the treatment plan. Typically there is also an appeal procedure.

Supporters claim UR achieves two goals. First, UR companies keep their screens current with the medical literature, something no physician or hospital could possibly do with the hundreds of studies published annually. Second, they claim that UR reduces inpatient costs by about 10%. (18)

Detractors see UR as an unwanted intrusion in the physician-patient relationship, with some physicians even lying to get around UR restrictions (19). Other detractors claim the UR companies have a financial bias to show cost reductions in order to get their contracts renewed. Interestingly this is the opposite of hospitals' financial bias to perform treatments—our second type of moral hazard, but in reverse?

An objective, unanswered question: do physicians complain because the clinical data don't support their proposed treatment plan—or because the UR firm cares too much about price?

Some commentators have concluded that UR has failed to provide the desired level of cost and quality control. The Journal of the American Medical Association reported a 'Retrospective Drug Utilization Review' study in 2003 that concluded 'we were unable to identify an effect of retrospective drug utilization review on...clinical outcomes.' (20). The New England Journal of Medicine reported that a studied utilization review program 'reduced the number of diagnostic and surgical procedures performed that required second opinions...(but) otherwise the program had little effect.' (21) The Canadian Medical Association Journal published a research study 'How valid are utilization review tools in assessing appropriate use of acute care beds?' and found that some UR companies underestimate—while others overestimate—appropriate hospital admission stays. (22). The CMAJ article concluded that

> Although utilization review tools are widely accepted, these considerations...raise serious questions about the value of the tools... and whether they should be used at all.

United Healthplan, for example, dropped Utilization Review from its managed care business in 1999, preferring physician policing to its UR overview. United Healthplan replaced UR with a fairly intensive effort to identify prospectively patients with chronic conditions that can be more effectively managed, and gives its data directly to each hospital. Other carriers eliminated UR practices that were costly to administer, irked consumers and providers, and failed to save much in terms of utilization. (23)

CONCLUSION

By the late 1980s indemnity health insurance looked sick indeed. US healthcare spending exceeded 10% of GDP with average spending increases per capita exceeding GDP annual growth per capita. The various cost and quality control programs achieved only some small successes and may inadvertently have added to healthcare system waste—by 1998 Medicare alone had 22,000 pages of regulation.

Some blamed the indemnity insurance structure. **The Economist** claimed that

> The inability of the fee-for-service (indemnity) system to provide good preventive care is arguably one of the main reasons why the average American is no fitter than, and lives no longer than, people from European or Asian countries that spend far less on healthcare' (24)

In fact, American diabetics were twice as likely to go blind or have limbs amputated as British diabetics because the British National Health Service 'worked harder to make sure they took their insulin injections and turned up regularly for eye tests'. (25) American children under 2 years old were less likely than Chinese to receive inoculation against diphtheria, tetanus, measles, mumps, rubella and polio. (26)

Yet the American healthcare bill continued to rise. The DRG experiment proved how strong and resourceful the medical billing sector was, while the UR experience showed the difficulties of outsider intervention in doctor-patient relations. Both of these failures rested on the American indemnification finance system, where the patients (customers) had such trust in their physicians. In other words, the American population seems to believe that physician trust is more important than healthcare cost.

The real winner under indemnity health insurance was moral hazard—the system that induced providers to bill. Every year healthcare premiums rose, but more people purchased health insurance. Every year healthcare spending rose, but our population didn't get proportionally healthier. Every year we added new technologies, medications and medical breakthroughs, but only a little to life expectancy.

The underlying reason for this contradiction was the indemnity finance system that rewarded providers for sick visits. The sicker the patient, the more providers could bill. There was little profit in preventive treatment as there was little for providers to do—give people a pill, an injection, some advice and send them packing. But for sick people—providers could develop technologies, medications, procedures, tests and protocols. There was money in this. The sicker the patient, the more providers could intervene and the more money they could make. Why intervene with a low cost treatment if something more expensive existed—especially with cost-plus reimbursement.

This frustration led to exploration of alternative healthcare finance options and to the growth of health maintenance organizations. Perhaps HMOs could reorganize healthcare priorities, control moral hazard, improve healthcare quality and control healthcare spending.

Chapter 2: Notes

1. See Kaiser Family Foundation website (www.KKF.org) 'Trends and Indicators in the Changing Healthcare Marketplace' for example.

2. David Dranove, The Economic Evolution of American Healthcare, Princeton University Press, 2000, page 33. Much of the conceptual outline and analysis, and several examples in this chapter—especially about PSROs, PROs and UR—come from this book.

3. Dranove suggests a fourth type of provider induced moral hazard also—that 'in extreme cases' physicians might even ignore unambiguous clinical indications to pursue their own financial goals. I do not believe that this constitutes a significant percentage of US healthcare expenditures.

4. A. Scitovsky and N. McCall 'Coinsurance and the Demand for Physician Services' Social Security Bulletin 35, number 6, 1977: 3—19

5. National Health Insurance Experiment

6. Dranove and Cone 'Do State Rate Setting Laws Really Lower Hospital Expenses?' Journal of Health Economics, 1985

7. Dranove, Economic Evolution, page 51

8. 'Keep Taking the Medicine' The Economist, July 15, 2004

9. Dranove, Economic Evolution, p 25

10. Ibid., p 58

11. Ibid. Preface to the paperback edition, page x.

12. CBO Testimony: Statement of Robert D. Reischauer, Deputy Director, Congressional Budget Office before the Subcommittee on Oversight, Committee on Ways and Means, US House of Representatives, June 27, 1979

13. Ibid.

14. Dranove, Economic Evolution, pp. 78—79

15. J. Wennberg, J. Freeman, and W. Culp 'Are Hospital Services Rationed in New Haven or Over-Utilized in Boston', Lancet 1 (1987): 1185-88

16. See also Dartmouth Atlas of Health Care, ed. Jack Wennberg (Chicago: American Hospital Publishing, 1996, 1999) which shows variations in a wide range of treatments, diagnostic tests and drug therapies. And G.O'Commer et al., 'Geographic Variation in the Treatment of Acute Myocardial Infarction' Journal of the American Medical Association 281 (1999): 627-33

17. Phelps, C, Health Economics. Reading, Massachusetts: Addison-Wesley,1997

18. T. Wickizer et al 'Does Utilization Review Reduce Unnecessary Hospital Care and Contain Costs?' Medical Care 27 (1989): 632-47

19. V. G. Freeman et al, 'Lying for Patients: Physician Deception of Third Party Payers', Archives of Internal Medicine (1999):2263-70

20. Sean Hennessy et al 'Retrospective Drug Utilization Review, Prescribing Errors, and Clinical Outcomes' Journal of the American Medical Association, Vol. 290, No. 11, September 17, 2003

21. Stephen Rosenberg et al 'Effect of Utilization Review in a Fee-for-Service Health Insurance Plan', New England Journal of Medicine, Volume 333:1326-1331, November 16, 1995

22. Norman Kalant et al 'How Valid are Utilization Review Tools in Assessing Appropriate Use of Acute Care Beds?' CMAJ, June 27, 2000: 162(13)

23. Joyce Frieden 'Insurers are loosening up on utilization review requirements' OB/GYN News, September 15, 2002.

24. 'Your Money or Your Life', The Economist, May 5, 1998

25. Ibid.

26. Ibid. Only about 75% of American children received these inoculations vs. some 90% of Chinese children.

CHAPTER 3
Moral Hazard in Managed Care

A second strain of health insurance developed at about the same time as Baylor University Hospital began working with the Dallas school system. In Los Angeles, Dr. Sidney Garfield offered Henry Kaiser—owner of several industrial and construction businesses—the following: For $.05/employee/day, Garfield would cover industrial medical care (workers comp) for all Kaiser employees. For an additional $.05, Garfield would also provide non-job related medical care.

Garfield and Kaiser established the Kaiser Foundation Health Plan, built medical facilities and, by World War II, had over 200,000 employees covered. After the war, Kaiser allowed non-employees to enroll also. As the medical insurance operation grew, Kaiser contracted exclusively with the Permanente Medical Group, Permanente worked exclusively with Kaiser members and this entity became commonly known as Kaiser-Permanente.

Kaiser-Permanente operated under a very different model from Baylor University Hospital. It owned its own hospitals to eliminate conflict between hospitals interested in occupancy and carriers interested in cost control. Kaiser hired physicians as salaried employees rather than fee-for-service contractors—a direct attack on moral hazard. Kaiser emphasized prevention, which was a reversal of the Baylor model and was designed to help keep costs down, and provided physicians and hospitals with financial incentives to keep people healthy.

This system evolved, and by the 1950s Kaiser-Permanente reported 25% shorter hospital stays than the US average. By the late 1960s, Kaisers' ratio of outpatient visits to hospital admissions was 50% higher than the US average. Other, similar Health Maintenance Organizations—the term coined to describe these plans—in New York City, Seattle and Illinois reported similar statistics.

Dr. Cecil Cutting, director of the Kaiser-Permanente Medical Group in northern California claimed in 1971 that the 'direct relationship of prepayment to providers becomes an incentive for the physician to develop economics in spending the medical dollar while maintaining quality' (1). And the Henry J. Kaiser Foundation attributed Kaiser's successes to 'the absence of a fee-for-service incentive to do what, by judicious surgical standards, constitutes unjustified surgery'. (2) By 1970 some 30—40 prepaid group practices were established nationally and were noticed by the medical and political communities. All the while, national healthcare costs continued to rise, almost tripling from $27 billion in 1960 to $73 billion in 1970.

The Nixon administration tried to tackle this problem head-on. Robert Finch, then Secretary of Health, Education and Welfare warned Congress in 1969 that 'the nation is faced with a breakdown in the delivery of health care unless immediate concerted action is taken by government and the private sector'. (3) The Nixon administration's solution became known as the HMO Act of 1973.

The Act was a political compromise. On one hand 'progressives', including Senator Ted Kennedy of Massachusetts, Governor Nelson Rockefeller of New York and the 1969 National Governors Conference wanted a national health insurance plan. Republican moderates, including Elliot Richardson who became Secretary of HEW, wanted the plan to encourage free market competition to keep costs down. And the American Medical Association opposed any changes from traditional fee-for-service medicine, prompting Kennedy to state in the Congressional Record, 1970 that 'there is perhaps no institution more resistant to change than the organized medical profession'.

The Act itself sought to promote a pre-paid healthcare system that would motivate doctors and hospitals to control costs and keep patients healthy. It was inexpensive to implement, costing the Feds $325 million to assist HMO development over 5 years (Kennedy and Richardson wanted $3.9 billion). However, the Act called for a loose physician structure that allowed doctors to opt-in or out, belong to multiple organizations or continue traditional fee-for-service medicine.

This ran counter to the Kaiser model of full time employee physicians, fully integrated into the clinical and hospital facilities—a key to Kaiser's cost control and preventive medical orientation.

Though Nixon's HMO Act of 1973 gave federal government legitimacy to Health Maintenance Organizations for the first time, it also inhibited HMO development by including burdensome regulations and only limited financial assistance. One unintended effect of the Act was inhibition of HMO development; though 124 HMOs developed between 1970—74, only 40 developed between 1974—78.

The market, however, responded differently, for businesses demanded more cost efficient medical services. Now that HMOs appeared 'legitimate', MBAs with access to investment capital began to see them as attractive for-profit vehicles. (Interestingly, this coincided with hospitals inviting MBAs to manage their DRG problems, described in Chapter 2.) The industry simply ignored Nixon's HMO Act, with it's federal funding tied to burdensome regulations. This was the second unintended consequence of the Act—the growth of for-profit HMOs using Wall Street capital rather than federal grants.

By 1986 only 41% of HMOs were non-profit (down from 88% in 1981). From 1985—1990 some 90 non-profit HMOs were organized. During the same period, some 300 for-profit HMOs were organized. By 1990, 33 million subscribers enrolled in over 600 HMOs. This would almost double to 60 million subscribers by 2000. The share of people getting employer based health insurance joining managed care organizations rose from 27% in 1988 to 92% in 2000.

HOW HMOs CONTROL SPENDING

HMOs use a combination of **selective contracting, payment capitation, pre-authorization, utilization review** and **diagnostic related groups** to control spending. (4)

In Kaiser-Permanente's classic HMO model the carrier, hospital and physicians were all the same company. This eliminated conflict between carrier desires for cost control and hospital interests in room occupancy. Full time physicians worked in autonomous, self-governing group practices, with fully integrated clinical, hospital and laboratory facilities. Each medical group received payment based on a capitated reimbursement system. This system avoided provider billing incentives that accounted for much of the moral hazard costs of indemnity health insurance.

Over time, however, these billing incentives returned. The same split between financier (insurance carrier) and providers that we saw in indemnity coverage also occurred with managed care.(5) This split reflected consumer demand for wider provider access and allowed moral hazard to re-emerge.

Carriers attempted to control costs initially by **contracting selectively** with providers, based on price. Carriers threatened providers with loss of business, for carriers could steer patients away from high priced physicians and hospitals.

Selective contracting worked quite well until about 2000 for one primary reason: a national excess of hospital capacity. According to Gordon Norman, VP of Pacificare, a large California-based HMO, this excess capacity was due to hospital overbuilding in the 1980s (6) making it easy for carriers to selectively contract with hungry hospitals. Hospitals offered price concessions (volume discounts) in return for patients. This addressed (somewhat) moral hazard and unnecessary care issues due to relatively strong carrier oversight.

Thomas McCarthy (7) notes that hospitals became more efficient during this period, with falling lengths of patient stays and more outpatient procedures. Cost-plus reimbursement was 'out'. Carriers contracted selectively and stipulated fees. Hospitals responded (as economists could have predicted) by merging and reducing excess beds. They also began affiliating with large physician practices to keep referrals coming.

After about 2000, consumers fought back. They demanded more choice among providers forcing some HMOs to consolidate. The more than 600 US HMOs of 1990 shrunk to some 500 by 2000. The effect of these trends—consumer demand for wider access, hospital consolidation due to excess capacity and carrier consolidation—was a return to healthcare inflation. (8)

More consumer choice meant broader provider networks with fewer gatekeepers, making HMO steering less effective. As power shifted to hospitals, they demanded higher reimbursement, less risk, better terms—and more opportunity for moral hazard mischief.

The US Federal Trade Commission noted this problem in an antitrust lawsuit win against Northwestern Healthcare of Illinois in 2004/5. (9) The FTC claimed that carriers, not patients, were the hospital's principal customers, for under managed care, few patients could chose their own hospital due to HMO selective contracting.

The Court found that Evanston Northwestern Hospitals' promises to lower prices through merger efficiencies never materialized. FTC attorney Thomas Brock said that this decision 'simply recognizes that with managed care and selective contracting, hospitals compete for the insurer's business' and hospital consolidation raises prices. And Ogan

Gurel, Chicago physician and President of Aesis Research Group said that there's an ebb-and-flow to the power relationship between hospitals and payers. Payers dominated in the 1990s and hospitals dominated in the 2000s.

Carriers, of course, responded to higher hospital payment requirements by raising premiums. The post-2000 combination of consumer demand for wider access and increased hospital bargaining strength ended the carrier's selective contracting cost control power. Just as moral hazard had defeated DRGs, so it defeated selective contracting as a cost control measure.

Carriers also tried to control costs by **capitating** provider reimbursements. The carrier would pay each provider a fee to cover all medical services for the carrier's customers within a specified area. This places providers at financial risk, and turns traditional fee-for-service reimbursement upside-down. Now the least busy physician or emptiest hospital may become the most profitable and expensive medical technologies may become liabilities rather than assets.

Capitation also eliminates need for utilization reviewers by allowing the capitalist market structure to work. Providers act more like other free-market producers of goods and services, concerned about maximizing revenues and minimizing cost of goods—all while maintaining high quality output. Theoretically, capitation induces more preventive medicine such as annual physicals, mammograms, pap smears, PSA tests and immunizations.

Also theoretically, capitation aligns provider incentives with patient needs. If a hospital discharges patients too early (to save money), the patients may end up costing much more upon return for an (unnecessary) second visit. Physicians who profit by underserving will ultimately lose when sick patients return. 'Under capitation, the foxes may be guarding the henhouse, but they are also responsible for egg production.' (10) And moral hazard is kept to a minimum.

Unfortunately, there are also theoretical disadvantages to capitation. Providers' economic incentives to undertreat may be very tempting, especially in the short run. Remember that a 10% increase in number of surgeons leads to a 2% increase in surgeries. Might the reverse also be true—that a 10% reduction in surgeons leads to a 2% reduction in (necessary) surgeries, thus putting patients at risk while providers enjoy higher than predicted profits?

If capitation levels are too low, providers may be unable to fund sufficient preventive care. Or, especially if subscribers can move easily from carrier to carrier, providers may have an economic interest in ignoring preventive care—as the patient may move to another carrier and provider before the economic effects of prevention become evident. And, if there are many available in-network physicians, an unscrupulous doctor may intentionally provide inadequate care, thus inducing sick patients to go elsewhere (and get treatment on another physician's dime). Or physicians receiving capitation reimbursement may select only healthy patients. This may make good economic sense, as very sick patients might bankrupt a provider.

How has capitation worked in practice? The **New England Journal of Medicine** reported on a three-year study in California comparing capitation to fee-for-service providers. (11) NEJM found that the number of inpatient days per 1000 non-Medicare subscribers was approximately 135 with capitated reimbursement compared to 232 for all California patients.

Though capitation may make good economic sense, it apparently does not make such good customer service sense. **Managed Care Magazine** found that

> Consumer satisfaction with HMOs is negatively correlated with the percentage of practitioners who are compensated on a capitated-fee basis and positively correlated with the percentage of practitioners compensated with a fee-withholding incentive (e.g. a fraction of fees that are withheld until specific quality and cost-control goals are reached). (12)

Managed Care suggested that over time, patients of salaried or capitated providers receive less medical care than fee-for-service providers…again, our definition of moral hazard. Capitation ran into the same problems as DRGs and selective contracting—that patients demand all the medical choice, options and treatment available when they have insurance. Patients vote with their feet (and pocket books) to maintain unfettered access. Moral hazard wins again.

Interestingly, PBS Frontline reported that 'capitation is stalling out as a payment method in many markets, as physicians and hospitals find that they very often lose money on capitated contracts, and go back to discounted fee-for-service payment whenever possible, instead.' (13) Apparently, neither providers nor consumers much like this healthcare finance method.

An alternative to capitation is a required **pre-authorization** for specialist services. This system is specifically designed to control moral hazard, for patients can only get specialist medical treatment when deemed necessary by their PCP and carrier. Further, the physician referral system is designed to ensure that each patient sees an appropriate, PCP selected and carrier approved specialist, providing both cost and medical quality controls.

Unfortunately, the referral system typically fails to control costs because PCPs fear two specific outcomes. First, the PCP may fear a lawsuit for professional negligence by failing to refer a sick patient to a competent specialist. Second, the PCP may fear that the patient will simply switch PCP unless the referrals are easy to obtain. In either case, referrals become an additional overhead cost to the system rather than a cost-reducing activity.

Carriers responded to consumer demands for easier specialist and treatment choice (especially post-2000) by easing referral requirements. By 2006, physician referrals in Massachusetts had become so routine that medical office managers often handled this entire process by telephone. No face-to-face interaction with patients, no PCP involvement—and little cost or quality control.

Yet even this level of referral requirement proved too burdensome for much of the American public, who have flocked to PPO (Preferred Provider Organizations) or POS (Point of Service) plans since the mid-1990s.

Plan Type	Percent of US Health Insurance Policies by Year (14)		
	1996	2000	2005
HMO	31%	29%	21%
PPO/POS Combined	42%	63%	76%

PPO and POS plans have no referral requirements for in-network physicians and typically cost about 15% more than comparable benefit levels in HMOs. In other words, the insurance carriers will charge consumers more for plans with fewer restrictions. The growth of these plans indicates how much the public objects to restrictions on physician,

GARY FRADIN

hospital or treatment choices in spite of the costs...or how highly consumers value their opportunity for moral hazard.

This returns us to Kaiser Permanente—respected for controlling its healthcare costs while providing outstanding medical care. Kaiser has long maintained its traditional HMO character—employee (not fee-for-service) physicians, tight referral control and low subscriber deductibles to encourage preventive care. As healthcare costs rose post-2000 and US consumers demanded wider access to providers, Kaiser maintained its traditional model. Now that might be changing.

In May 2006, Kaiser introduced Choice Solution, a policy allowing small-business employees to choose among plans that allow members to see providers outside the Kaiser system, marking the first time this option became available to small businesses. Kaiser also introduced some high deductible plan options. 'If Kaiser is moving in this direction, that's really the last bastion of the comprehensive, low-co-pay, low cost-sharing benefit' claimed Jill Yegian, director of health insurance for the California Healthcare Foundation in Oakland (15). Dennis Lum, Kaiser's vice president of channel strategy and systems said that Kaiser didn't want to lose its traditional, integrated service delivery focus, but 'today, given the more complex marketplace we're in...we have to find a way to address what we perceive as a very powerful trend.'

Just like our Miami Medicare recipients demanded specialists for every body part, so Kaiser subscribers demand freedom from tight managed care restrictions. They want more care options and more physician treatment flexibility even, apparently, if this means higher premiums. Perhaps our experiment with managed care has highlighted a consumer trade-off: when faced with a choice between more flexibility or lower premiums, consumers chose flexibility...and then complain about the high premiums!

EFFECTS OF MANAGED CARE

Initially the HMO movement achieved positive cost control results. From 1993—1999,US healthcare inflation averaged about 2.4%. Managed care organizations enrolled approximately 92% of workers getting healthcare from their employers by 2000; traditional indemnity coverage had practically disappeared.

Employers liked the cost controls imposed by HMOs, for these controls kept health insurance expenses low. Consumers complained about restrictions on physicians and care and demanded more choice, options and alternatives. And, just as happened with the Baylor University Hospital model, some carriers responded to consumer demands, loosened restrictions, allowed more consumer choice—and moral hazard returned, along with healthcare inflation.

After 2000, inflation returned to double digits annually, with health insurance premium increases averaging 15%+ from 2002-2004. The hospital capacity excess of the 1990s disappeared just as carriers loosened consumer restrictions. From 1990 to 2000, healthcare expenditures grew from 12.6% to 14% of US GDP, or an average of .14% above the GDP average annual growth. From 2000—2004, healthcare expenditures grew from 14% to 15% of GDP, an average of .25% above the GDP average. Medicare expects healthcare to cost 18.7% of GDP by 2014—a projected average annual growth rate of .37% faster than GDP average annual growth.

In other words, the rate of healthcare cost increases as compared to the average growth of US Gross Domestic Product will triple from the mid-1990s to the mid-2010s. Much of this is caused by our healthcare financing structure and control system that allows increased consumer choice, physician options and hospital power. We as a society have voted at every opportunity for fewer consumer healthcare restrictions and more opportunity for moral hazard even as we beseech our politicians to 'do something about healthcare'.

The Economist summarized our 1990s managed care experiment in 2004 by claiming it only 'treated the symptoms' of healthcare inflation, just like every other cost control strategy. 'What started as a revolution turned out to be mainly a mechanism for insurers to secure price discounts from physicians and hospitals.' (16)

Every year, our brokerage agency informs clients at renewal of their new healthcare rates. Since about 2000, as rates have risen by double digits, our clients have had a uniform reaction: 'This is ridiculous. They should do something about it.' "They" presumably means politicians and regulators.

President Bush, in his first term and while running in the 2004 election, had two major healthcare proposals. First, he introduced 'Health Savings Accounts' as part of the Medicare Modernization Act of 2003. These were designed to increase consumerism in healthcare purchasing as a means to control healthcare expenditures.

Second, he introduced legislation promoting 'Association Health Plans' to allow small businesses to band together and negotiate better healthcare rates with insurance companies and providers.

In the next chapter, we'll consider both of these ideas and see how they compete with moral hazard for their place in our healthcare system.

Chapter 3: Notes

1. C. Cutting, 'Historical Development and Operating Concepts,' in The Kaiser-Permanente Medical Program, ed. A Somers (New York: Commonwealth Fund, 1971). Reported in David Dranove, The Economic Evolution of American Healthcare page 40
2. G. Williams, 'Kaiser-Permanente Health Plan: Why it Works' (Oakland California: Kaiser Foundation, 1991), also in Dranove, p 40
3. 'Health Care Warning', Congressional Quarterly Weekly Report, July 18, 1969, page 1271
4. This chapter will discuss selective contracting, capitation and pre-authorization. See Chapter 2 for discussion of DRGs and utilization review. Again, many concepts and examples come from David Dranove, op. cit.
5. Kaiser, however, maintained its original structure of salaried, employee physicians and Kaiser owned hospitals at least until 2006, when, for the first time, it began contracting with out of network providers.
6. 'Keep Taking the Medicine', The Economist, July 15, 2004
7. T. McCarthy 'Hospital Contracting Practices' National Economic Research Associates 3/27/2003
8. See Martin Gaynor, 'Consolidation can push prices up, not down', RAND Journal of Economics, Vol 34, 2003. Gaynor shows that mergers can push hospital prices up by 50%!

9. Reported in Modern Healthcare, Kellogg School of Management, January 2, 2006

10. J.D. Kleinke 'Bleeding Edge' Aspen, 1998

11. New England Journal of Medicine, December 1995, 'Study of the Effects of Capitation in California, 1990—1993'

12. Managed Care magazine, 2006 'Effect of Practitioner Compensation on HMO Consumer Satisfaction'

13. PBS Frontline, aired April 9, 2000. See Mark Hogland, 'Dr. Solomon's Dilemma' at www.PBS.org

14. Kaiser Family Foundation 'Trends and Indicators in the Changing Health Care Marketplace', www.KFF.org

15. Victoria Colliver, 'Kaiser Redesigns its Health Plans to Better Compete' San Francisco Chronicle, September 24, 2006

16. 'Keep Taking the Medicine' The Economist, July 15, 2004

CHAPTER 4
Moral Hazard Under President Bush's Healthcare Proposals

After winning the Presidency in 2000, President Bush put his stamp on our healthcare system by proposing two major modifications to managed care: Health Savings Accounts and Association Health Plans. Health Savings Accounts (HSAs) became law in 2003; Association Health Plans have not (late 2006) been enacted.

HEALTH SAVINGS ACCOUNTS DESCRIBED

President Bush launched a direct attack on moral hazard when Health Savings Accounts became law in 2003. HSAs are specifically designed to make healthcare more like other economic goods and to inject more consumerism into healthcare purchases. HSA policyholders spend their own money (initially) on healthcare. This, according to HSA proponents, will induce them to shop more wisely, consider various treatment costs, avoid unnecessary procedures and lower our national healthcare inflation rate.

HSAs are comprised of two separate but linked components—a high deductible health insurance plan with an optional tax-advantaged savings account. The IRS defines 'high deductible health insurance plans' as having an individual annual deductible between $1100 - $2850 and a family annual deductible between $2200 - $5600 (in 2007). These deductibles are indexed and adjusted annually. The insured pays the entire deductible before the carrier pays anything. Once the insured reaches the annual deductible most or all medical services are fully covered by the carrier. (1)

The Health Savings Account legislation also allows the policy subscriber to establish an optional, tax-advantaged 'health savings account'. HSAs look and act much like Individual Retirement Accounts. Subscribers can invest up to their annual IRS allowed amount in a triple tax-free account, the only triple tax-free investment vehicle allowed by the IRS. HSA investments can be pre-taxed (not included in the subscribers' adjusted gross income for tax purposes), accrue interest tax-free and be withdrawn tax-free, provided the funds are spent for IRS approved medical purposes. (2)

As the Health Savings Account grows over time, the subscriber can purchase a higher and higher deductible health plan at, presumably, lower and lower premiums, and thus gain control over health insurance premium inflation. The subscriber will also have more (personal, saved) money to spend on healthcare. HSA proponents hope this will give consumers more economic power in the healthcare marketplace.

To enhance consumer power, HSAs typically rest on a PPO, not HMO chassis. HMOs typically require Primary Care Physician referrals as a cost-control mechanism and restrict consumer choice of specialist. PPOs (Preferred Provider Networks) typically do not require such referrals for in-network specialists and charge higher premiums than HMOs for this consumer flexibility. Health Savings Accounts typically charge lower premiums than PPOs but do not require referrals for in-network specialists or treatment. Instead of using referrals to control costs, HSAs use high deductibles as a cost-control mechanism with proponents believing that consumers will avoid unnecessary treatment and will shop wisely for specialists. (3)

THEORY OF HEALTH SAVINGS ACCOUNTS

Health Savings Accounts seek to use economic market forces to control healthcare spending and improve healthcare quality. HSA theory rests on three key economic assumptions.

First, health savings accounts alter the underlying nature of managed care for the good of consumers. (4) The pre-HSA US tax structure subsidized comprehensive, high premium / low deductible health insurance. Premiums were tax-deductible to employers but not income taxable to employees, providing incentives to purchase high-premium, low deductible plans. This amounted to a $100+ billion subsidy for the medical industry and directly contributed to the medical arms race and moral hazard excesses.

The traditional insurance structure drives medical innovation toward new, expensive technologies. Consumers demand this, taxes subsidize this and Wall Street finances this. There are no significant provider incentives to focus on cost reduction or low cost treatment alternatives. The only traditional managed care-based cost control options are provider restrictions—network restrictions, time restrictions (physicians overbook) or denial of services.

HSAs offer distinct advantages. Tax advantages are switched to employees, for deductibles become tax-free. It now makes sense to purchase lower premium, higher deductible plans. Reducing premiums puts more money in employee pockets. Pre-HSA, employees would have paid approximately 45% of their premium savings in taxes (27% Federal, 15% State payroll and 5% State income) negating much of the lower-premium advantages. The HSA 'triple-tax-free' benefit rearranges this and provides an inducement for employees to switch to lower premium, higher deductible plans.

Second, proponents assume that market forces will make providers more price competitive as they seek to attract consumer dollars—much like other producers of economic goods and services. Proponents hope, for example, that MRI diagnostic centers will compete based on price, advertise 'specials' and act more like car dealers.

They hope other providers will also specialize in discrete medical treatments and become low cost producers of these. Some providers, for example, will specialize in organ transplants while other will specialize in orthopedics and still others in cardiac procedures—much like producers in other economic fields. By specializing, hospitals will gain both expertise and efficiency, outcomes will improve and prices will fall. Providers will compete based on price and quality, and consumers will shop wisely.

When HSAs become widespread (according to proponents), the medical arms race will end, moral hazard will decrease and competition among providers will reduce healthcare costs and improve quality.

Third, proponents hope that consumers will make lifestyle adjustments to lower their medical costs. They hope that HSAs will provide consumers with economic incentives to practice healthier lifestyles and thus avoid need for medical treatment. The HSA finance structure will induce consumers to save money by avoiding medical treatments.

HSA proponents see potentially huge economic savings from lifestyle changes. Blue Cross and Blue Shield of Massachusetts listed some **Tips for Better Health** just as HSAs became law. (5)

Eat balanced meals for weight management. The US CDC estimates that excess body fat costs the US $31 billion annually for treatment of overweight people who develop heart disease;

Exercise daily. The CDC claims that direct medical costs associated with physical inactivity in 2000 exceeded $75 billion. Also if 10% of adults began a regular walking program we would save $5.6 billion in heart disease medical costs;

Quit smoking. Smoking costs $68 billion in direct and indirect costs annually;

Chose generics whenever possible. The Blue Cross Blue Shield Association estimates a $10 billion potential annual saving by switching to generics.

Traditional managed care provided no economic incentives to avoid medical treatment, for medical visit copayments were very low. By increasing the costs of medical care, HSA proponents try to put healthy lifestyles in consumers' economic interests.

DO HEALTH SAVINGS ACCOUNTS WORK?

Some 3% of all insured employees purchased Health Savings Accounts nationally in 2006, up from 1% in 2004. (6) In Massachusetts, Tufts Health Plan, the first to introduce HSAs in the Massachusetts market, discontinued its Liberty Plan in 2006 due to lack of subscription. (7)

Though touted as 'lower premium plans' HSA premiums were often not low enough to induce many subscribers to switch from traditional managed care plans to these new high deductible plans; consumers perceived too much deductible risk vs. premium savings.

Here is an example of my personal individual health insurance rates, comparing Harvard Pilgrim HMO and HSA options, effective December 1, 2006:

Carrier Name	Plan Name	Office Co-pay	In Patient Deductible	HSA Annual Deductible	Monthly Premium
Harvard Pilgrim	Aff 25 HMO with Rx	$25	$1000	N/A	$510.36
Harvard Pilgrim	Aff 25 HMO no Rx	$25	$1000	N/A	$440.36
Harvard Pilgrim	HSA 1500	$20	N/A	$1500	$449.42
Harvard Pilgrim	HSA 2000	$20	N/A	$2000	$423.18

I used the Affordable 25 with Rx as HMO reference point, as this is currently the most popular Harvard Pilgrim HMO for small businesses according to our agency data.

The $2000 deductible HSA costs $87/month less than the Affordable 25 HMO with Rx—an annual premium savings of $1044. Against this savings is the $2000 deductible risk. Most consumers perceive better value in the HMO. Though tax benefits and individual risk analysis may improve the HSA attractiveness, the HSAs still fail to provide a compelling economic case for purchase.

HSA consumers also need information about provider costs and outcomes, to ensure that they spend their deductible wisely. This information is insufficiently available and comprehensible for consumers to make wise, informed decisions. 'We're in a world where everything is behind the curtain,' says Charlie Baker, CEO of Harvard Pilgrim Health Care in Massachusetts in 2004. (8) Blue Cross Blue Shield of Massachusetts, for example, posts Sleep Study prices as ranging from $50—$500; or a Child Emergency Room Visit ranging from $310—$470. How is a consumer to use this information? Which local hospital is highest and which lowest—that information is unavailable. (9)

Even if we knew all treatment prices, Dr. Meredith Rosenthal of Harvard's School of Public Health asks a different question: 'Who wants bypass surgery from the cheapest surgeon in town?' (10) The perceived risk of poor treatment outcomes motivates most people to want the best, not cheapest surgeon. And, as discussed in Chapter 1, we currently lack objective data to help consumers determine which surgeons are the best and which are below average. Absent such data, and fearing unlimited risk from using a poor surgeon, consumers often equate price with quality. Some routine medical treatments—perhaps diagnostic or non-invasive procedures—might be appropriate for price shopping, but certainly not (patient-perceived) potentially life threatening ones.

HSA design allows consumers to invest up to their annual deductible in triple-tax free savings accounts so consumers can purchase high and higher deductible plans over time without increasing their financial risk. Presumably consumers will use part of their annual tax-free deductible for medical purposes and invest the rest. (11) This benefit may be mis-targeted.

Epidemiological data indicate that young people have lower rates of medical expense than do middle aged or elderly folks. People in their 20s and 30s will more likely <u>not</u> use their entire annual deductibles, so will have money left over for investment in their personal health savings account. These young people will also have the longest time horizon for their HSA account to compound interest and grow. People in their 50s and 60s are <u>more</u> likely to use their annual deductible for medical purposes. Even if they invest in health savings accounts, they have less time for their money to grow.

Unfortunately, young people tend to have less disposable income than over-50s. When faced with student loan repayments, saving for house downpayments or starting a family, young people are less likely to invest their annual deductible in long-term health savings accounts. Also the tax advantage to young, lower income workers is less valuable than to higher income people. A $2000 tax deduction may be worth $1200 to a high-income person but only $800 to a low-income employee.

Thus the HSA incentive structure is out-of-line with its targeted populations. Young people might enroll in high deductible health plans but be unable to participate in the long-term tax advantaged savings accounts. Older people have little economic incentive to participate in either part of Bush's program: though they may have more disposable income to invest, they have less time for their investments to grow. And they are more likely to spend their annual deductible on healthcare. As a tax and investment vehicle, HSAs miss their targets.

But perhaps the chronically ill population and unequal distribution of medical care pose the worst problem with President Bush's Health Savings Accounts program. The US Centers for Disease Control estimate that 70% of US healthcare costs pay for chronic conditions such as diabetes, high blood pressure or heart disease. (12) Many chronically ill have on-going annual medical expenses that would exceed their annual

HSA deductible. Once they reach their deductible all (or most) care becomes free, depending on specific HSA plan design.

For the subscriber who annually exceeds the deductible, HSAs look more attractive than traditional HMOs. HSAs—post deductible—have neither the office visit or hospitalization copayment, nor the PCP referral requirement, of HMOs. HSAs—post deductible—offer more moral hazard opportunities than do traditional indemnity or managed care coverage.

See the chart, below, for an estimate of US medical cost distribution. (13)

Percent of US Population	Percent of Medical Expenditures
1%	24%
5%	49%
10%	64%
50%	97%

The bottom (healthiest) 50% of the US population accounts for only about 3% of medical expenditures.

Ten percent of our population consumes about 2/3 of our medical expenditures. This averages approximately $7000/person—way over the HSA annual deductible. (14) These people could pay their HSA premiums and annual deductible and then all medical services become (essentially) free. Their annual medical expenses so exceed the IRS allowed deductible that shopping or other cost controls become irrelevant.

Thus about 2/3 of total US medical expenses fall outside the HSA cost control scope. And this 10% of the US population is unaffected by the moral hazard restrictions imposed by Health Savings Accounts. For this group of consumers, HSAs are irrelevant.

Where might HSAs work? For the 50% of the population that represents 3% of US healthcare costs. This group might take advantage of premium reductions and save money shopping wisely for medical treatments. And a percentage of this group—the young, healthy and financially capable—may contribute annually to their individual Health Savings Account and prosper.

But will this affect total US healthcare costs very much? Unlikely. Even if this half of the population cut its healthcare costs by a third, this would represent a decrease in total US healthcare expenditures of about 1%.

Once again, moral hazard trumps control. The small percentage of our population that is chronically ill and demands a high level of medical service will be unaffected by President Bush's attempts to make healthcare more like other consumer goods. They will continue to demand high levels of service, continue to pay their (relatively small) office and hospitalization copayments and continue to allow physicians to bill fee-for-service. Providers treating this group still have no financial incentive to offer good preventive or low cost treatments and little financial incentives to offer anything other than expensive, technologically advanced treatments. Patients have little financial incentive to practice healthy lifestyles or to avoid treatment altogether. But all parties can access medical interventions that add little to longevity or quality of life—exactly the moral hazard problems discussed in Chapter 1.

President Bush's first attempt to control healthcare costs looks likely to fail due to demographics and moral hazard. Let's look now at his second plan, the national introduction of Association Health Plans.

ASSOCIATION HEALTH PLANS

President Bush wants to allow groups of small businesses to band together for purposes of negotiating health insurance rates. He supports the **Small Business Health Fairness Act** (H.R. 4281) that would

> 'create association health plans (AHPs) to allow small businesses to join together through bona-fide trade associations to purchase health insurance for their workers at a lower cost. The measure would increase small businesses' bargaining power with healthcare providers, give them freedom from costly state-mandated benefit packages, and lower their (healthcare related) overhead costs by as much as 30 percent'. (15)

The Association Health Plan Coalition, comprised of 100+ US business associations, claims that Association Health Plans will 'make coverage more affordable by spreading risk among a much larger group, strengthening negotiating power with plans and providers, and reducing administrative costs.' (16) AHP proponents claim that small businesses currently pay higher premiums than do large corporations for the same benefit levels. By banding together, the association of small businesses will become attractive to providers, who will discount their prices for access to this large group of potential customers.

Association Health Plan theory runs counter to most managed care cost control theory. Most current cost control comes from <u>supply</u> constraints—selective contracting, capitation, PCP referral requirements, DRGs or utilization review. AHP theory focuses instead on <u>demand</u>, suggesting that demand characteristics—either group demographics or group size—will lead to savings.

Some commentators question this demand-based assumption. (17) A select population <u>may</u> have lower disease rates than the general population, thus reducing medical costs and AHP premiums. (The general population exhibits 'average' medical costs. If your population deviates from the norm, you may deviate in an advantageous—or disadvantageous—way; this follows from the definition of 'average'.) If the select population has unexpectedly <u>high</u> disease rates, however, this may drive up AHP medical costs and premiums, and likely drive the AHP out of business. (18) H.R 4281 specifically 'prohibits AHPs from charging higher rates for sicker individuals or groups within the plan'.

Presumably association members will compare their AHP premiums to regular, non-AHP market prices. If the association population deviates disadvantageously from the norm, AHP rates will rise. Members will then switch to (cheaper) non-AHP plans and the AHP population pool will likely shrink, perhaps forcing the AHP out-of-business.

The American Academy of Actuaries also doubts that AHPs can achieve sufficient <u>size</u> to negotiate particularly attractive rates from providers, flatly stating:

> It is difficult to create a scenario that would result in any AHP being able to realize the critical mass of members that would allow them the leverage to negotiate the deeper discounts that large HMOs and insurance companies currently enjoy with providers. (19)

Currently, hospitals have strong power in rate setting, as argued in Chapter 2. Hospitals have a symbiotic relationship with large carriers—both need the other. As such, hospitals and large carriers set reimbursement rates together.

Seventy two percent of Massachusetts' consumers currently get the rates negotiated by the following carriers:

Carrier	Approx. # of Subscribers	Approx. % of Mass market
Blue Cross Blue Shield	2,600,000 subscribers	45%
Harvard Pilgrim Health Care	1,000,000 subscribers	17%
Tufts Health Plan	600,000 subscribers	10%

Groups lobbying for Association Health Plans in Massachusetts include:

Massachusetts Nursery and Landscape Association—1078 members
American Physical Therapy Association of Massachusetts—1800 members
Massachusetts Association of Land Surveying and Civil Engineers—700 members
Massachusetts Funeral Directors Association—500 members
Massachusetts Association of Realtors—15,000 members (20)

In Massachusetts, as in many other states, hospitals have banded together for purposes of protecting their reimbursements. Partners HealthCare, which dominates the eastern Massachusetts hospital market and owns Massachusetts General Hospital, Brigham and Women's Hospital, Faulkner Hospital, Newton-Wellsley Hospital and the North Shore Medical Center, has the most lucrative insurance contracts in the state (21). Indeed, as argued in Chapter 2, Partners has been 'unabashed about flaunting (its) power, publicly stating (its) intention to use (its) leverage when negotiating rates' (22).

The large Massachusetts carriers, notably Blue Cross and Harvard Pilgrim, act as counterweights to Partners' desires to raise rates. It is difficult to see how the American Nursery and Landscape Association Health Plan, with its 1078 Massachusetts members, or the National Funeral Director's Association, with its 500 Massachusetts members, will negotiate better rates with Partners than Blue Cross (with 2.6 million members) or Harvard Pilgrim (with 1,000,000).

Commentators also question the administrative savings claims of AHP proponents. If AHPs staff up to fill all the same administrative functions as typical managed carriers—including sales, marketing, underwriting, enrollment, billing, provider services, etc—then finding opportunities for administrative savings seems difficult. AHPs might 'rent' administrative services from other insurance carriers. This would, presumably (AHP proponents fail to spell out specifics here) be priced at 'cost plus'; the insurer would charge the normal administrative fee 'plus' a small rental fee. Again, little obvious opportunity for administrative savings.

Indeed, the American Academy of Actuaries states bluntly that 'administrative expense savings have not been realized' by association health plans in past incarnations. (23)

Blue Cross Blue Shield of Massachusetts spends 7+% of premium on administration and 2+% on cash reserves, totaling under 10% of premium for administration and cash reserves. (24) Average Massachusetts's health insurance premiums per capita run approximately $6500/year (25). At 10%, the annual per capita administrative fee is $650. A 15% administrative cost reduction by an association health plan would translate to savings of about $97.50/policy/year, or a 1.5% premium reduction. Hardly worth the effort, especially as premium inflation runs about 6—9% annually. Consumers would likely not even notice the difference.

Yet Association Health Plans offer one tantalizing attraction to small businesses that current managed care plans do not—the ability to waive state mandates and thus reduce premiums. This, claim AHP proponents, is the crux of the issue. Small businesses should be free to choose an 'appropriate' benefit level for their employees and not be required to comply with all state requirements—just like large corporations do.

AHP proponents want national AHP regulation from the U.S. Department of Labor to supercede individual state requirements.

This creates the fatal flaw in association health plan theory. All AHP proposals before Congress require that both the association and member be 'bona fide'—that the association exist for years prior to offering health insurance, that the association exist for reasons other than to offer health insurance, and that the association member be 'in good standing' or the equivalent. (26)

Yet most associations constantly seek new members. Most have a 'Membership Director' whose job description entails membership expansion. I, for example, in the past 5 years have been a paid-up member 'in good standing' of well over a dozen business associations, including the Cape Cod Cranberry Growers Association, the Massachusetts Auto

Body Association and my local Chamber of Commerce. I could, therefore, join an association health plan sponsored by any.

But if I could join, virtually anyone else could also join. There are few, if any, barriers to entry. This would allow each association—demographically and epidemologically—to resemble the general population. And the medical risk profile of any association could match the general population.

However, if the Department of Labor regulates AHPs while each individual state regulates non-AHPs, then AHPs simply become a mechanism for avoiding state mandates and consumer protections for any state resident!

Health plans that waive state mandates and consumer protections could (fairly easily) offer lower prices than plans that comply with all regulations. AHPs could be limited benefit plans—not cover cancer treatment, for example. (In Massachusetts, state regulated HMOs cover all medically necessary treatment—clearly much more expensive.)

Or AHPs could have stringent 'pre-existing condition' exceptions. (In Massachusetts, state regulated employer-based HMOs have NO pre-existing condition exceptions—clearly much more expensive.)

Or AHPs could have annual benefit coverage maximums. (In Massachusetts, state regulated HMOs have NO annual benefit coverage maximums—clearly much more expensive.)

Actuarial data indicate that healthier people are less likely to utilize mandates and therefore more likely to enroll in AHPs. (27) People with higher health risks and higher utilization of mandated services are more likely to remain with traditional state-regulated plans. With fewer healthy people in state regulated plans, medical expenses for the traditionally insured group will increase, as will premiums.

This will create a gap in price between carriers complying with state mandates and AHPs. The healthy population will gain, but the less-healthy population will lose. The net effect of introducing AHPs with state mandate waivers will likely be about zero—the price reductions to some small businesses will offset the price increases to others.

Having some health plans comply with state mandates while others do not will create consumer confusion. Consumers may well think that plans offer the same—or almost the same—benefits, with some carriers simply controlling costs better than others. This has been our agency experience.

Some health plans cover, for example, <u>all</u> inpatient costs, while others cover only <u>allowable</u> costs—a subtle but potentially very costly difference. The Boston Globe reports (28) on such plans offered in Massachusetts. These plans cap hospital room and board coverage at $400 per day (even though actual costs approach $2000/day), physician visits at 1 per day at $100 (even though some specialists charge more), office visits at $50 and inpatient charges at $12,000 (regardless of actual charges). The Massachusetts Attorney General sued one company in October 2006, alleging that the company used deceptive marketing and improperly denied patient claims. The Globe reports that these health plans 'contain a confusing mix of deductibles, copayments, and coverage maximums on physician visits, hospital stays and tests' that harm consumers.

AHP subscribers may not realize until time of claim which plans include state protections and which do not; insurance agents can obfuscate this difference and insurance policy fine print is notoriously difficult to read. Customers will likely be upset to learn that they in fact lack the coverage they thought they had. Indeed, the Globe reports (29) on Erin Chartier who faces about $50,000 in medical bills that she thought were covered by her 'affordable' health insurance. 'It's affordable because they don't cover anything,' she says—though she only learned this after-the-fact.

An AHP limited benefit plan may offer consumers a stark choice: lower premiums with lower benefits (and presumably fewer provider options) or higher premiums for all state mandated benefits, more provider choice and more consumer protections. Consumers faced this choice with HMOs in the late-1990s and early-2000s and voted overwhelmingly— they want more benefits, richer plans and more provider options. HMOs responded with wider physician networks, fewer referral restrictions—and more opportunity for moral hazard. Now AHPs want to re-create history by designing plans with (potentially) even fewer consumer options than the HMOs of the late-1980s and early-1990s…and significantly fewer consumer protections, though these are likely to be camouflaged.

The current AHP proposals may result in three major unintended consequences that could harm consumers and providers (30):

> Association health plans may be unable to provide the required premium savings unless they get state health care mandate and consumer protection law waivers. This waiver will likely harm consumers;

AHPs may be able temporarily to offer lower rate health insurance rates through the elimination of state mandates. However, the benefit limitations and rate structures in those AHPs may lead to rate increases for traditional, mandate-compliant carriers and thus long-term increases in the uninsured population—i.e., the unhealthy non-association members who can no longer afford coverage;

AHPs are not expected to generate higher provider discounts and lower administrative costs to produce lower premiums on a sustainable, long-term basis, than the premium rates currently available to small groups.

An association health plan bill passed in the Republican controlled House of Representatives in 2003, but never reached the Senate floor. With the recent switch to Democratic control of Congress, federal AHP legislation prospects appear unclear.

CONCLUSION

President Bush's two healthcare proposals—Health Savings Accounts and Association Health Plans—seem doomed to fail. Neither aims to improve healthcare quality and neither appropriately addresses the underlying reason for high healthcare premiums—moral hazard.

Yet the American healthcare buying public still clamors for lower premiums. The public still wants someone to do something about healthcare costs.

Maybe, rather than designing new cost control mechanisms or developing new types of health plans, we should look elsewhere to see how other countries deal with their healthcare costs—and combat moral hazard. Other countries have different healthcare experiences than we do. Let's look at Britain, to see if their single payer National Health Service has answers that could help us.

Chapter 4: Notes

1. The IRS allows variations on the basic high deductible plan. Some plans call for 100% coverage for covered services after deductible for 'in-network providers' but less for 'out-of-network

providers'. All approved plans include pharmacy copayments even after the deductible has been reached.

2. HSA savings accounts are heavily regulated. For detailed information on IRS regulations, read 'All About HSAs', US Treasury Department, November 28, 2005 or visit www. hsainsider.com.

3. Note that HSAs implicitly assume that consumers can make informed medical choices. See Chapter 1, especially the discussion of consumer diagnostic perils and PCP referral patterns.

4. Much of this discussion comes from Martin Feldstein, former Chairman of the Council of Economic Advisors under President Reagan and Professor of Economics at Harvard, as outlined in the Wall Street Journal op-ed section, January 19, 2004.

5. Blue Cross Blue Shield of Massachusetts 'Choices' consumer magazine, Winter, 2003

6. Boston Globe, November 20, 2006, page E4.

7. Tufts enrolled about 10,000 subscribers from 2004—mid-2006.

8. Boston Globe, May 29, 2004 page A6

9. Ibid.

10. Lecture at Tufts Health Plan, January 11, 2005

11. Some commentators have suggested that rational consumers will avoid preventive medical treatments and invest their entire deductible. They will only practice preventive medicine in years that they exceed their deductible, so the preventive services are fully covered by their carriers and become 'free' to the consumer.

12. Blue Cross Blue Shield of Massachusetts, ibid.

13. William, W. Yu and Trena M Ezzati-Rice 'Medical Expenditure Panel Survey Statistical Brief #81', May, 2005, Agency for Healthcare Research and Quality

14. For these calculations I assumed $2 trillion in US annual medical expenses and a US population of 280 million.

15. Bill Summary 'Small Business Health Fairness Act (H.R. 4281): Improving Access to Quality Health Care for Uninsured Families', House Education and the Workforce Committee, John Boehner, Chairman, May 13, 2004

16. Letter to Chairman Boehner urging support for H.R. 660, undated. See www.asme.org/NewsPublicPolicy/GovRelations/PositionStatements
17. See FAQs on AHPs, American Academy of Actuaries Issue Brief, March 2005
18. This is the basic insurance 'law of large numbers'. A carrier insuring 100,000 lives can absorb an unexpected large loss more easily than a carrier insuring 100 lives.

If the AHP is small but suffers higher than expected medical expenses, its premiums could increase and become higher than those of other carriers. Then, depending on renewal regulations, the healthy might exit the AHP, leaving only the unhealthy to remain. This would create a death-spiral of AHP rate increases, flight by healthy members—and more AHP rate increases to cover the (increasingly large) percent of unhealthy members. This scenario underlies the failures of the following AHP-type programs, reported at the Luncheon Briefing, May 14, 2004 of the American Academy of Actuaries, 'Is there strength in numbers? Will AHPs work?':

- Sunkist Growers of California which became insolvent in 2001. Had covered 23,000 people. Left $11 million in unpaid claims;
- New Jersey Coalition of Automotive Retailers which became insolvent in 2002. Had covered 20,000 people. Left $15 million in unpaid claims;
- Indiana Construction Industry Trust, which became insolvent in 2002. Had operated since the 1960s. Had covered 22,000 people. Left $20 million in unpaid claims.
- Licensed Beverage Association of New Jersey, which became insolvent in 2003. Had covered 1000 people. Left $2 million in unpaid claims.

19. American Academy of Actuaries, Issue Brief, March 2005.
20. These are the Massachusetts affiliates of national associations that support association health plans. Massachusetts's membership statistics came either from the Massachusetts association website or from telephone calls to the Massachusetts office.
21. Boston Globe, January 2, 2007, page D3

22. David Dranove 'The Economic Evolution of American Healthcare' Princeton University Press 2000, Preface to the paperback edition, page x.

23. 'Is there strength in numbers? Will AHPs work?' American Academy of Actuaries, Luncheon Briefing of the American Academy of Actuaries, May 14, 2004

24. Reported in the Blue Cross Blue Shield of Massachusetts's spring 2004 broker seminar.

25. Based on our agency's internal data. Our average small group—under 5 insured employees—annual 2005 premium was $6,435. This compares to Hewitt Associates average of $7999 per capita as reported in the Boston Globe, August 2, 2005, page A5.

26. Bill Summary, op cit., page 2.

27. American Academy of Actuaries 'Issue Brief' March 2005. This section comes primarily from the answer to question 'Will AHPs provide similar benefits to those provided by other health plans in the states where AHPs operate?'

28. Boston Globe, October 31, 2006 'Low-cost insurer leaves bills and a bitter taste' by Christopher Rowland, Business Section

29. Ibid.

30. American Academy of Actuaries 'Issue Brief'

CHAPTER 5
Moral Hazard in Single Payer Systems:
Case Study of the British National Health Service

While American healthcare consumes about 15% of our Gross Domestic Product, the British National Health Service only consumes about 8% of British GDP. The British have longer life expectancies than Americans—- 1.5 years longer on average. British infant mortality rates are lower than ours. Perhaps the British have learned how to control moral hazard and deliver good healthcare for a fraction of our price; perhaps they have found the answer. (1)

SOME BACKGROUND

The British National Health Service (NHS) is a 'single payer system' where the government funds healthcare for all Britons. Most countries have single payer systems — the United States and South Africa are the 2 major counter examples.

Single payer systems share some common characteristics:

1. All providers receive funding from the same, single source;
2. Medical care is free (or almost free) at the point of consumption;
3. All residents receive the same health benefit levels. The NHS mantra is 'free at the point of delivery, provided on the basis of need.' (2)

Single payer systems offer the attractions of

- Equity—all residents are covered and treated alike,
- Simplicity—all residents have the same health benefits, and
- Low costs—including all residents spreads healthcare costs over the widest possible population and lowers costs per unit. This is the basic 'law of large numbers' concept that underlies all insurance.

According to surveys, almost 60% of Americans think a government managed single payer system would work better than our current 'managed competition.' (3)

Single payer systems use annual, national budgets to control spending. In Britain, Parliament determines the national healthcare budget, then allocates resources by autonomous geographic region. Each region allocates annual resources by provider, with hospitals getting the bulk of funds. And each hospital allocates annual resources by department.

Budgets remain in place for a year, until the next annual budget begins the process all over again. In general, each annual budget is a fairly small percentage change (generally increase) over the previous budget. Hospitals have difficulty growing at much above the annual inflation factor irrespective of medical need, hospital specialty or hospital quality, for the following reason: the British regional health authorities have, for years, believed that controlling hospital staffing was the best way to control healthcare spending. The regional authorities simply lack the resources to promote huge hospital expansion projects.

Political considerations enter this budgetary process at several points. When Parliament sets that annual national budget, healthcare lobbyists complete with other lobbyists for their share. They compete, for example, with educational lobbyists, environmental lobbyists, transportation lobbyists, foreign aid lobbyists, defense lobbyists and others for part of the national budget. Parliament allocates public moneys among these various necessary public functions.

Only part of Parliament's consideration includes actual demand for health services. Besides healthcare demand, Parliament also considers competing needs for public funds, the political power of each lobby and the availability of resources. The final national budget presumably reflects the 'will of the people' rather than demand for specific medical treatments and technology investments.

With so many hospitals competing for regional resources, one hospital's increase (above trend) generally comes at another hospital's expense. This rigid budgetary system can allow for political trading that is unrelated to medical demand or need. Conceptually, one hospital may exchange a two-year cardiology investment for another hospital's two-year urology decrease—and then reverse or modify the trade in the future. Note that hospital investment becomes both a political and medical needs issue.

After the regional authority makes its hospital funding decisions, then each hospital allocates funding by department. Here the political influence of department heads and senior specialists (called 'consultants' in Britain) becomes important. Some commentators refer to this as a 'semi-feudal system' with consultants, rather than hospital administrators controlling the key funding decisions. The nephrology department may have more political clout than the neurology department and may thus gain at neurology's expense, almost without regard to relative need.

Demand for specialist services is controlled by General Practitioners (GPs)—the British equivalent of our Primary Care Physicians. GPs act both as medical practitioner and budgetary gatekeeper, regulating patient access to specialists. NHS patients (generally, traditionally) can only access certain hospitals and related specialists: neither GP nor consumers have had system wide hospital choice, though this is changing. (4)

In 2004 Britain had 35,000 GPs, averaging 1600 patients each. (Primary care physicians in Massachusetts averaged about 700 patients in 2006.) Ninety percent of all NHS contacts went no further than the GP in the early 2000s.

However, other political and financial considerations may take precedence over GP referrals. **The Observer**, a respected British weekly newspaper, reports (November 5, 2006) that

> Thousands of patients are being denied access to hospital consultants because the NHS has set up money-saving management schemes (that) block GPs' referrals...Patients with rheumatoid arthritis, knee problems and eye and skin conditions are being targeted by managers who intercept referral letters and send them back to GPs rather than allowing them to be seen by the appropriate specialist...
> **In north London, all outpatient follow-up appointments are being stopped unless the patient has cancer.** (Emphasis added)

The NHS budgeting system allows so much political influence that some observers conclude:

> 'The NHS is in crisis, leading to tens of thousands of unnecessary deaths each year...fundamental reform is needed...to address the root cause of the problems of the NHS—that it is a politically controlled state monopoly that is institutionally unresponsive to the needs of patients' (5)

What happens when resource constraints or political considerations enter the healthcare budgetary process and supercede demand as an allocation parameter? We will examine how the British National Health Service deals with excess demand in terms of <u>waiting lists</u>, <u>equity</u>, <u>technology investment</u> and <u>systemic priorities</u>.

<u>WAITING LISTS</u>

'Waiting is widely associated with publicly funded health care systems; it indicates the absence of costly excess capacity'. (6)

In 1999, over 1,200,000 patients were awaiting inpatient or outpatient treatment in England; Ireland, Wales and Scotland had longer waits. (9) By 2001 this had declined to only about 1,000,000. Of these, over 43,000 had been waiting more than a year. The Adam Smith Institute estimates that people currently on NHS waiting lists will collectively wait about one million years longer to receive treatment than doctors deem acceptable. (7)

The Observer reports that delays for colon cancer treatment are so long that 20 percent of these cases considered curable at time of diagnosis are incurable by the time of treatment. Twenty-five percent of British cardiac patients die while waiting their turn to receive treatment. According to government reports, one in six people on NHS waiting lists for elective surgery are removed without ever being treated. And between 1999 and 2001, 36% of British adult surgery patients had to wait more than 4 months for non-emergency surgery, compared to 5% of American adults. (8)

In response to these long waits, many Britons obtain private health insurance, sometimes supplied as a benefit to key employees. In 2000, some 7 million people (about 11% of the population) had private policies. Most people buy these policies to avoid waiting for medical service. In Britain 'you pay to avoid waiting, or wait to avoid paying.' (9) Some 20% of all surgeries are performed in private hospitals or private beds in NHS hospitals. The private sector specializes in the 'three Hs'—hips, hernias and hemorrhoids, along with some elective surgery, particularly gynecologic and ophthalmologic. (10) Twenty percent of British hip operations are private, as are about 50% of abortions. (11)

However, private coverage is predominately obtained by upper income Britons, primarily in southeastern England near London: some 22% of 'professionals' and 23% of 'employers and managers' had private coverage in 2000, compared to 4% of Scots. (12)

This public / private system allows abuse. Consultants (specialists who control public hospital resource allocations and also work at private hospitals) can control waiting lists. It may be quicker to see the same consultant privately than wait on the NHS list. Or consultants can move preferred patients to the top based on medical or non-medical criteria.

Some specialists have even altered treatment protocols to increase their income. Cardiologists for example may find a partially blocked coronary artery while performing an angiogram. Standard US practice is to perform angioplasty at that time. This reduces the patient risk of two catheter insertions and two anesthetics. It is also more time efficient. But some NHS cardiologists inform the patient, upon waking, of this blockage and then reschedule the angioplasty—with the related lengthy NHS waiting period. The cardiologist may also tell the patient of quicker operating room availability at his private clinic. This is far more lucrative for the cardiologist as the NHS does not regulate private compensation.

The waiting list problem has degenerated to such an extent that **The Observer** reported (October 1, 2006) on people injured in the July 7, 2005 subway terrorist bombings who had still not been treated at NHS hospitals, even after 15 months. 'We were supposed to be made an NHS priority, but only a handful of specific survivors with extreme injuries have been fast-tracked' claimed survivor Beverli Rhodes.

Rather than continue waiting, Rhodes plans to join the 10 survivors who have so far received medical treatment in Thailand (!). Forty more survivors plan to follow. One survivor, quoted a price of 100,000 British pounds for private treatment in the UK is being charged only 7,000 pounds for the same procedure in Bangkok.

EQUITY

As political factors influence medical resource allocation, areas in Britain with the most political clout get the best medical facilities. The wealthier areas around London have the highest ratio of medical services per capita, and poorer sections of, for example Scotland, have the lowest. This has led the British press to refer to the 'postcode lottery' in which a person's chances of receiving timely, high quality treatment depend on the neighborhood or 'postcode' of residence. (13)

'The Good Hospital Guide', which grades every hospital in Britain on a mortality index, confirmed one indicator of this postcode lottery. Hospitals in wealthy sections of London rated highest on patient mortality scales, while hospitals in the poorest sections rated lowest. London's top 10 hospitals, ranked by mortality, average 52 physicians/100 beds, while the 10 worst average only 31 physicians—a 40% difference! (14)

Britons suffering from renal failure and living in southeastern England have much better access to kidney dialysis centers than others. London has 11 centers within 5 miles of each other and (wealthy and politically important) southeastern England has 16. The rest of the United Kingdom—including all of Scotland, Wales, Northern Ireland and most of England—has only 28 dialysis centers. London and southeastern England have half of the kidney dialysis centers in the UK—but only 26% of the population. (15)

In Scotland, working class Glasgow and western Scotland receives far less than it's fair share of medical services. (16) Glasgow has only 8 cancer specialists per million of population; wealthier Edinburgh has 13. Glasgow's Beatson Hospital, Scotland's largest cancer treatment center serving about 2.7 million people in western Scotland has 7 specialist radiotherapy machines; Edinburgh and eastern Scotland with about half of this population, has 5. (The US averages 6 radiotherapy machines per million people. To match the US average, Glasgow would need 16 machines and Edinburgh 7.) Beatson's underfunding results, according to **Observer** reporter Arnold Kemp, from

> 'The systematic discrimination against Glasgow from politicians and administrators in Edinburgh that dates from about 1990. The then Scottish Secretary Malcolm Rifkind told me that the substantial public investment in the west of Scotland paid the Tories no political dividends.'

Apparently no political payback on election day means little public investment in cancer treatment for Glasgow residents.

TECHNOLOGY INVESTMENT

Britain increased its rate of CT scanners per million of population almost 7 fold between 1981 and 2001. This resulted in approximately 25% as many CT scanners per million population in Britain as in the US in 2001. (17)

Number of CT scanners, US and UK per 1 Million of population

	1980	2001
US	6.5	29.4
UK	1.1	7.1

The US National Institutes of Health recommend that every hospital with 200+ beds and a diverse caseload have a CT scanner. The US reached this level in 1985; Britain in 2006.

The British have been reluctant to invest in new, expensive technologies until those technologies have proven their worth. This clearly reduces the chance of large investments in unproven technologies, or resources wasted in promising, but ultimately ineffective technologies. The bureaucratic, rigid British healthcare budgeting system resists embracing new technologies.

British NHS bureaucratic budgeters look for a technology financial return on investment. They ask a simple question: is the Return On Investment (ROI) of CT scanners so much better than X-ray or ultrasound as to justify the huge investment? (They could invest alternatively, for example in expanded dermatology services.) It is difficult to answer this question satisfactorily—and rapidly—for conservative bureaucrats with new technologies. As a result, the British have severely lagged behind American medical breakthroughs, and British treatment protocols sometimes seem almost archaic to American physicians.

We can note three effects on the National Health Service of British failure to invest in CT technologies in the 1980s.

First, the lack of CT scanners reduced perceived demand for information generated by this technology. With weak demand, the British invested fewer resources in training radiologists. As a result, even after the British began budgeting for more scanners, they faced the human resource constraint of an insufficiently trained radiology community. Films were often read by less well-trained radiographers.

Second, the lack of scanners and trained radiologists meant that diagnosticians were unable to specialize in different organs. The US developed radiology specialties in the mid-1980s: chest radiologists, GI radiologists, neuroradiologists—and even subspecialties such as invasive neuroradiologists and non-invasive neuroradiologists. The British, by contrast, either relied on a 'radiology generalists' or on older, less sophisticated diagnostic tools such as X-rays and ultra-sound until recently.

Third, waits for CT diagnosis extended to almost unbelievable periods. British reports of waiting periods for non-life threatening (though potentially very painful) conditions such as lumbar back or knee problems extended to 10—24 months.

We can postulate that new technology diffusion in single payer systems is slower than in the American system. Americans spend more on technology, often choosing to invest when the British would watch, wait and consider the ROI versus other investment options more carefully. Clearly the Americans will sometimes get it wrong and invest unwisely.

But a more fundamental question underlies this technology discussion. How would American consumers react if our medical system adopted the British 'go slow' approach to new technologies? Would Americans with painful joints or suspected cancers accept that 'we can't offer you the latest diagnostic technology because we're unsure it's ROI, so we'll use an older, less dynamic, less clear, less certain diagnostic tool'?

I think that Americans always want the best, the latest, the clearest, the most robust technology available when their health is at stake. More on this later.

SYSTEMIC PRIORITIES

The British have made a fundamental healthcare finance choice that differs from Americas. The British have decided that, due to severe financial constraints, they will accept a 'modified utilitarian' (my term) approach to healthcare investment.

We will define 'modified utilitarian' in two ways. First, in the classic 'greatest good for the greatest number' without spending too much on healthcare. The British believe that resources are finite, and that they must protect the financial strength of British economic society by investing only an 'appropriate' amount in healthcare. This may cause some sick or elderly to receive sub-optimal treatment—apparently an acceptable price to pay for economic stability. Most people get adequate medical care. The overriding public investment goal is the financial stability of British society.

This philosophy resonates in Gordon Brown's 2005 'Chancellor of the Exchequer's Budget Statement' (18):

- 'My Budget choice is to lock in stability and never put it at risk'
- 'Our first fiscal rule is to balance the current budget'
- 'I firmly believe that a shared British national purpose (is)... that we never...take risks with stability'
- 'Stability the foundation'

This contradicts the American medical approach, which we can summarize as 'do as much as possible for everyone' even if this includes paying the highest healthcare prices in the world (by a large margin). American medical malpractice lawyers, for example, make their livings by showing where providers failed to provide appropriate treatment for each individual. American society is far more individual-centric than Britain.

Our second definition of 'modified utilitarian' somewhat contradicts the first. We can state this as 'Exceptions to rule #1 exist when high profile or highly publicized medical failures may have significant negative effects on the Government.' The British try to invest in medical procedures that limit the number of publicly seen sick children or other situations that might make the Government look bad. By contrast, the British limit investments to sick elderly who likely will not appear in newspapers.

We can demonstrate this 'modified utilitarianism' by contrasting the British healthcare investment in kidney dialysis and hemophilia. (19)

BRITISH KIDNEY DISEASE TREATMENT

Kidney failure allows toxins to accumulate in the body. Untreated, kidney failure can lead to death. There are two main types of treatment: dialysis and transplant. And there are two main types of dialysis: hemodialysis and peritoneal dialysis.

In hemodialysis, the patient's blood flows via a catheter into a blood-cleansing machine. Treatment takes several hours, several times per week in a dialysis center. Hemodialysis has good treatment success rates. This increases demand for machines and dialysis centers as people live longer and thus need their machines longer. In 2005, British hemodialysis costs averaged about $45,000 per patient per year. (20)

Peritoneal dialysis can be home based. It is much cheaper. Here a special solution is inserted into the abdominal cavity via a plastic tube. Waste products move into the solution by osmosis and then exit the body. The fluid is periodically drained and replaced. This requires a very low NHS investment—typically just a monthly solution refill and an occasional check-in from an NHS visiting nurse. However, peritoneal dialysis can put significant time and skill demands on the patient's family. If these are inappropriately managed, the patient's treatment may suffer.

Kidney transplants, typically costing about $25,000 in 2005 are the most complex of options. Transplants require a donor, a highly skilled medical operating staff, hospital resources and a sufficiently ill patient to warrant the medical risks. One constraint on transplants: number of available donors. (British law until recently imposed restrictions on kidney donations from strangers.) British transplant rates have sometimes been higher than US rates. One suspected reason: the inadequacy of home supports for peritoneal dialysis, which results in unsuccessful treatment and need for life saving transplant surgery.

Dialysis centers operate on fixed annual budgets without regard to patient demand. This provides financial incentives for nephrologists to prescribe peritoneal (home) dialysis or transplant.

Dialysis and Transplant Rates, US and UK 1980 and 2002
1980 - # procedures per million population

	US	UK	
Hemodialysis	190	60	
Peritoneal Dialysis	3	9	(Peritoneal is 13% of UK dialysis total
Transplant	42	56	but only 1.5% of US total.)
Total	249	128	(UK does 51% of US total)

2002 - # procedures per million population

	US	UK	
Hemodialysis	978	244	
Peritoneal Dialysis	86	92	(Peritoneal is 27% of UK dialysis total
Transplant	424	289	but only 8% of US total.)
Total	1496	625	(UK does 42% of US total)

In the 1980s, British treated patients up to age 44 at about the same rate as other western European countries, but treated few over 50 and almost none over 55. Interestingly, the British believed that they provided optimal care at this time. They believed that over-55's were 'a bit crumbly' and inappropriate for care. They also rejected diabetics or people with co-morbidities. The British attitude can be summarized by this nephrologist, making a statement to a child of a 65 year old suffering from renal failure in the 1980s:

> 'I would say that your mother's kidneys are failing and there is little anybody can do about it because of her age and general physical state, and that would be my suggestion or advice that we spare her any further investigation, and further painful procedure, and we would just make her as comfortable as we can for what remains of her life.'

This nephrologist apparently believes that societal resources can best be spent elsewhere; that the potential longevity or life quality gains for this 65-year-old are insufficient to justify the medical cost. The NHS suffered in the 1980s from very tight budgets and scare financial resources. This nephrologist practiced the British modified utilitarian philosophy.

By 2002, NHS funding levels increased and nearly 50% of new British dialysis patients were over 65 years old. Apparently, the elderly respond better to kidney treatment when funding becomes available!

Renal failure patients suffer privately. They may appear weak but generally otherwise look normal. Theirs is not a disease that attracts widespread public displays of interest, protest or comment. They receive treatment behind closed doors. When their illness becomes acute, they pass away fairly quickly without big public displays.

This is not the case for hemophilia.

BRITISH TREATMENT OF HEMOPHELIA

Hemophilia is a bleeding disease, usually diagnosed in children, that if untreated leads to suffering, disability and death. However, modern treatment—blood transfusion based—can allow hemophiliacs to have close to normal lives and life expectancies.

In the early 1980s, when Britain operated the National Health Service under very severe financial constraints, the average annual treatment cost per hemophiliac was about $6,000. This has grown to over $100,000 post-2000.

The total 2001 population of hemophiliacs in Britain was only about 6300. Of these, about 2300 were deemed 'severe' cases, which represented about 90% of the total approximately $290 million total hemophilia treatment costs...less than 3/10 of 1% of the total NHS budget.

The British treat almost all hemophiliacs according to need, apparently without regard to the severe budgetary constraints faced by renal sufferers. There seem three reasons for this. **First**, the relatively small number of hemophiliacs in the 1970s and 1980s, combined with the relatively low annual treatment costs, made treatment of the entire hemophiliac population inexpensive. Budget decision-makers **second**, seem to have decided in the 1970s and 1980s to treat this group fully, rather than allow the small hemophiliac population to suffer painfully and visibly. This budgetary decision apparently represents a public relations decision—a desire to avoid an adverse public reaction to letting young people suffer visibly. (The British hemophiliac population is relatively vocal, as evidenced by their loud public outcry over tainted blood used in transfusions in the early 2000s.) (21)

Third, changing the NHS policy, institutionalized over many years, became more difficult than offering hemophiliacs only partial treatment. As Aaron says, 'the willingness to pay what it costs to treat hemophilia may also reflect the emotive force of the stark symptoms of hemophilia compared to the quiet decline associated with renal failure.'(22)

In 2005, some 6,000 patients were still on kidney treatment waiting lists (23), while all hemophiliacs received appropriate treatment.

MORAL HAZARD AND SINGLE PAYER SYSTEMS

Our analysis of the British NHS as a single payer system example leads to one clear conclusion: healthcare cost control comes from restricting healthcare services. The British restrictions include:

- number of hospital employees, by the budgetary process,
- number of procedures, by annual budgets

- number of specialist visits, by GP referral power and hospital management procedures,
- number of medical tests, by waiting lists
- technology investment, by budgets

The British public and medical establishment, by-and-large, accept these restrictions even while complaining about the NHS. Britons seem to accept the modified utilitarian philosophy that economic conservatism and stability are more important than some excessive, potentially life-saving medical expenditures. As a British physician summarized attitudes of his colleagues:

> "If physicians over here had infinite resources, they would treat person-for-person less people than…in the US…a different attitude to end stage renal failure…I think (US dialysis rates are) just an example of modern interventional technology being misused" (24)

Americans demand more healthcare options. We have voted with our pocketbooks since the 1990s for fewer managed care restrictions, easier referrals and wider provider access, as argued in Chapter 3. Though we often complain about health insurance prices, we are generally loath to trade-off lower cost plans for tighter carrier restrictions.

In many ways, the British NHS looks like a capitated healthcare finance system—the kind that **Managed Care** magazine said (Chapter 3) lost favor among American healthcare consumers.

Would Americans embrace an NHS type single payer system even if it would cut our healthcare expenditures in half? I suspect not. I suspect that Americans, when faced with public waiting lists, healthcare inequality and slow embrace of new technologies would turn to the private sector for help.

We have demonstrated over the past 50 years that choice is our primary criterion in healthcare consumption: <u>we</u> want to choose our own doctor, hospital and method of treatment, and not have that choice imposed by the government or an insurance carrier. And we want our healthcare treatments now, on our timetable, not next year, on the governments'.

I suspect that imposition of a tightly controlled, budget-constrained single payer system in American would, almost by definition, stimulate the private sector to offer health insurance policies. I do not believe that American healthcare consumers would accept the modified utilitarian approach of Britain. We are too habituated to demand that we each individually receive all the treatment available, almost irrespective of price.

In other words, we demand access to moral hazard. We demand access to care, even if it may cost more than its worth. We demand access to expensive treatments even if lower cost treatments exist. We demand access to treatment plans that are even better than our primary care physician deems necessary. We demand access to specialists at Massachusetts General Hospital or the Cleveland Clinic or the Mayo Clinic even if our local hospitals' specialists are more appropriate.

Our demands for access, choice and excessive care would doom an NHS type, cost-conscious single payer system. Such a system would, almost by definition, become two systems: one funded publicly and the other privately, perhaps based on employment or employer contributions. Employers who want to attract and retain the best employees would offer the most attractive health insurance plans. Top employees would seek these employee benefits. And we would recreate a system much like our current one.

The basic problem Americans have with the British NHS is the restrictions: the reason the NHS works economically is exactly the reason most Americans would not like it. As such, it is an inappropriate solution to America's healthcare problem.

We have so far discussed the inability of indemnity health insurance, managed care, health savings accounts, association health plans or single payer systems to control American healthcare spending and improve our healthcare outcomes. We have argued that perhaps 1/3 of our healthcare resources are wasted on treatments that add little to longevity or life quality.

But we have not adequately addressed the question of American healthcare benefits. Do we, even in spite of the wasted resources and moral hazard, continue to get a good economic return on our healthcare investment? We'll discuss that in the next chapter.

Chapter 5: Notes

1.   There are various types of single payer systems. Rather than provide a purely theoretical analysis, I chose to offer a case study using the British National Health Service in this chapter. Clearly, the British NHS is a unique organization, with both advantages and disadvantages over the health services in other countries. I chose to evaluate the British system primarily because Britain is an advanced, industrialized country (like the US) and there is easy-to-access, good research information available about the NHS. Others could use examples from other countries and potentially reach conclusions different from mine.

   Much of the data and analysis in this chapter comes from Henry J. Aaron, William B. Schwartz and Melissa Cox 'Can We Say No?', Brookings Institution Press, 2005 and John C. Goodman, Gerald L. Musgrave and Devon M. Herrick, 'Lives at Risk', Rowan and Littlefield, 2004

2.   My thanks to Dr. Michael Gordon for this. Personal correspondence January 8, 2007.

3.   "Findings from 17 State Survey," America's Health Insurance Plans, April 12, 2004

4.   Severe GP referral restrictions, which limited treatment to the local hospital, were enacted by the Government in the 1970s. Some of these restrictions were lifted on January 1, 2006 when patients received the right to choose treatment from at least 4 hospitals and specialists.

5.   Anthony Browne and Matthew Young, 'NHS Reform—Towards Consensus?' The Observer, April 7, 2002

6.   Paul McDonald et al., 'Waiting Lists and Waiting Times for Health Care in Canada.' Health Canada, Summary Report, July, 1998, quoted in John C. Goodman et. al. page 21.

7.   This paragraph came from Goodman, et al , pages 21 and 23

8.   Ibid., except for the Observer information

9.   Gordon suggests another reason for private insurance—to see your consultant of choice, rather than whichever consultant your GP recommends, rather like American PPO policies.

10. Swu-Jane Lin, 'Developing Disease State Management in the United Kingdom', Journal of Managed Care Pharmacy, May/June 1998, page 281

11. Aaron, page 25—26

12. Aaron, page 161

13. Goodman, page 28

14. Goodman, pages 29—30

15. source: www.statistics.gov.uk

16. Arnold Kemp 'Ten Years of Ignoring Suffering', Observer, December 9, 2001

17. Aaron, page 82. Much of this section relies on Aaron's analysis.

18. HM Treasury, Chancellor of the Exchequer's Budget Statement, Speech March 16, 2005

19. Much of this analysis relies on Aaron, pages 30—50

20. This estimate comes from The Guardian, February 13, 2003 'Victory for Haemophilia Patients'. (Note that the British spell 'haemophilia', whereas Americans spell 'hemophilia'. I use the British spelling in direct quotes.) Aaron gives conflicting data on hemophilia treatment costs/person. See pages 49 and 111

21. For example, see James Meikle, The Guardian, February 13, 2003 'Victory for Haemophilia Patients'. Some 4000 British hemophiliacs had received blood tainted with HIV or hepatitis. The British Government 'sought to end a long-running dispute with the haemophilia community by finally putting all British patients on the same footing over access to synthetic clotting factor known as recombinant.' This governmental decision would cost approximately $125 million over 3 years.

22. Aaron, page 111

23. James Meikle, 'Donor Hunt to Ease Kidney Shortage', Guardian, May 31, 2005.

24. Aaron, page 44

CHAPTER 6
Valuing Healthcare Benefits

We have seen how moral hazard increases our healthcare costs by promoting inefficiencies. Inefficiencies, remember, are defined as medical interventions where the treatment costs exceed the benefits (as measured by increased longevity or quality of life) or economic considerations enter the treatment plan. We have seen how carriers, Medicare or Medicaid attempted—generally unsuccessfully—to control moral hazard. And we have seen that President Bush's attempts to control healthcare costs missed the moral hazard mark and failed.

As a result, medical costs have grown from $27 billion in 1960 to almost $2 trillion in 2006, and healthcare spending as a percentage of US Gross Domestic Product has increased from 5% to 16% during the same period. Medical insurance premiums rose from about $500 per capita in the 1950s (inflation adjusted) to about $5000 per capita today.

What have we purchased with this additional money? Have we spent the additional $4500 wisely? If so, perhaps healthcare is actually NOT terribly expensive even though it costs more today than ever in the past. If we spent the $4500 wisely and get a good positive return on investment, then healthcare might be APPROPRIATELY priced, or even INEXPENSIVE.

The concepts of 'expensive', 'appropriately priced' or 'inexpensive' are relational economic terms. 'Expensive' compared to what? If we compare 2006 healthcare costs to 1950 healthcare costs, then clearly today's costs are higher and more 'expensive'.

But if we compare today's healthcare Return on Investment to past healthcare ROI then we may get a different story. Perhaps healthcare investment is like college investment. College tuition is now much higher than in the past; but college graduates today earn significantly more than non-graduates with the gap widening. The ROI of a college education today may be even higher than the ROI many years ago when tuition was lower.

If healthcare ROI is high, indicating that we get excellent value from our healthcare system, then perhaps we need not worry unduly about costs and health insurance premiums. We get good value from our healthcare investments; these stimulate other sectors of our economy and the system works well. But if healthcare ROI is low, then perhaps our investment is poor, our healthcare system too expensive and moral hazard has damaged the economic value of this institution.

Clearly we have made healthcare gains in the past half-century. Life expectancy is higher and infant mortality lower. Our question becomes 'Have we received <u>enough</u> benefit from our healthcare investment? Is the healthcare Return on Investment still positive?' (1)

THE HEALTHCARE SITUATION OF 1950s

People who complain that healthcare is too expensive would, perhaps, like their $4500 back with a return to 1950s healthcare. At that time antibiotics were still new, but effective in reducing infection; hospitals became reasonable places to receive medical treatment, rather than breeding grounds for medical infection.

'Surgeons' performed all surgical procedures, with surgical subspecialties not recognized by the AMA until the 1970s. Many medical subspecialties had not yet been invented, including endocrinology (1971), hematology (1971), medical oncology (1972), critical care medicine (1985) and radiology for example.

In the 1950s, modern medical technology was in infant stages. Not yet invented: CT scanners, MRI machines, kidney dialysis, organ transplants, joint replacements, cancer surgeries, phototherapy for jaundiced babies—to name a few.

American life expectancy was about 68 years in the 1950s compared to about 80 years today, with several medical technology trends underlying these gains. Until about 1950, American life expectancy gains (measured as 'life expectancy at birth') resulted primarily from infant mortality rate reductions. In 1900, about 20% of children died before age 10; by 1950 about 10% died and today only about 3% die before age 10. Survivors of age 10 had little increased life expectancy from 1900 until the 1950s due to lack of infectious disease treatment. The introduction of sulfa drugs, penicillin and other antibiotics drastically reduced infectious disease rates by the 1960s. Post-1960s, most reduction in infant mortality rates became a function of survival of low-birth weight babies.

Also post-1960s, reductions in American chronic disease mortality added to our national life expectancy gains. Significant reductions in cardiovascular disease since 1960 have increased life expectancy of middle-aged people. Similarly, advances in geriatric medicine have increased life quality and expectancies of the elderly—our nursing home population has remained approximately constant during this period, despite major increases in the elderly population.

Though we have increased both our life expectancies and life qualities, we have done so at tremendous expense. Our question remains: Do we have a positive economic return on our healthcare investment?

ECONOMIC VALUES OF HEALTH BENEFITS

To value many healthcare benefits we need first to establish an economic value of life. Once we have this value, we can determine how much an additional year of life is worth—and how much we should invest to gain that additional time.

This sounds absurd—valuing a year of life. Valuing life involves ethical, religious, legal, political and economic issues, and makes us feel uncomfortable. I may value my life more highly than you value it; and you may value your child's life more highly than anyone else may. Our society may value a heinous criminal's life less highly than the President's. Or you may believe that we are all equally valuable before God and that life's value is priceless. These are very difficult questions to consider and I tread lightly when approaching the answer.

But if we are to allocate healthcare resources efficiently we need some outcome measure to help us—a common yardstick to measure, for example, the value of a $100,000 heart by-pass operation vs. a $1000 MRI scan. If both produce the same outcome value, then we could consider the $100,000 heart by-pass surgery an 'inefficient' resource use, or 'expensive'. Far better to purchase 100 $1000 MRI scans and gain 100 times the hypothetical by-pass result.

Our attempt to place an economic value on an American life (2) uses a methodology called 'willingness to pay' (3). This is the methodology used by David Cutler in 'Your Money or Your Life' and commonly accepted among academic economists. We will look at what Americans are willing to pay for various life-saving devices such as car air bags. We will then aggregate the air bag consumption decisions of our entire society and compare this to the number of lives saved by air bags. Since driving, automobile accidents and air bag expenditures affect a wide cross section of our population, this methodology may approximate an 'average' American's values. (4)

Air bags are now standard in new cars. When they were an optional purchase they cost about $300 each—some people purchased and others did not. Studies have shown that air bags save the life of 1 driver in 10,000. Paying $300 to save 1 life in 10,000 is the equivalent of paying $3 million for each life saved. (5) This air bag example indicates that, based on overall American consumption decisions, as a society we value each life at least at $3 million.

Interestingly, this $3 million life value based on air bag consumption is relatively consistent with conclusions from consumption studies of other life saving devices such as home fire alarms, home carbon dioxide detectors or boat life preservers. Economists who have used this methodology have concluded that—based on our consumption patterns—we value our remaining years between $3 and $7 million, with $5 million as an approximate average.

We say 'remaining years' as today's consumption decisions will affect our future years, rather than our total life years. (Buying an air bag today will have no affect on your previous life.) The US average life expectancy is about 80 years and our average age about 35 (6) so the average US consumer has about 45 years more to live.

Dividing the 'about $5 million' value of additional life by the 'about 45 years' more to live indicates that most Americans value each additional remaining life-year at about $100,000. (7) We will use this figure for ease of analytic use. (8)

Calculating the value of each additional life year is conceptually fairly simple, but quantitatively very complicated.

Analysts ask if each additional life year is worth the same amount. Some medical interventions keep people alive but in pain; others extend a depressing life; while still others extend an only partially fulfilling life. Economists try to measure Quality Adjusted Life Years (QALYs)—to measure health quality combined with longevity.

This term was first coined in the 1970s (9) and has stimulated an entire branch of medical economics that measures QALYs under difference circumstances. Basically QALYs assign values ranging from 0 (dead) to 1 (perfect health): values closer to 0 indicate poorer health, and closer to 1 indicate better health. Medical economists then rank healthcare interventions by QALY, with the lowest cost/QALY being the most efficient intervention. These are notoriously difficult calculations to make, are at best crude measurements and are based on trade-offs that most people prefer not to consider. (10) Here we will estimate QALYs conservatively in our attempt to value healthcare benefits.

We will make one other adjustment to our $100,000/additional life year estimate; we will adjust for social 'externalities'. Externalities occur 'when one person does something that influences the economic circumstances of others (so) the costs and benefits of that action for other people need to be taken into account.' (11).

Consider a disabled worker, currently collecting $30,000 in welfare benefits per year. If this person receives medical treatment that extends his life and eliminates his disability, society can save $30,000/year. This positive externality should be added to the $100,000 life year calculation, for now our society is $130,000 richer (the previously disabled person is $100,000 richer per life year and society saves $30,000 in payments to him).

Similarly, medical treatments that extend lives of elderly people living on state subsidies have a negative externality. At a $10,000 annual transfer payment per elderly person, our society gains only $90,000 in net life year benefit for each additional elderly life year ($100,000 benefit for the individual minus $10,000 cost to society of welfare payments). We will use some crude externality calculations in our analysis.

CASE STUDY: LOW BIRTH WEIGHT BABIES (12)

We begin our healthcare economic analysis by considering the costs and benefits of medical treatment of low birth weight babies.

Low birth weight babies weigh under 5.5 lbs. Thirty percent will suffer impairments ranging from cerebral palsy to blindness to mental retardation. Another 30% will have minor problems such as learning impairments or slow development. Low birth weight babies have a slightly lower life expectancy (about 70 years) than the US population in general.

In the 1950s, medical technology offered little help to low birth weight babies. Incubators modified from chicken incubation technology offered some help, as did fairly primitive provision of oxygen and warmth. Ventilators, phototherapy and steroid therapy (to speed up infant development) were all developed in the 1970s and 1980s. Some pharmaceuticals were developed in the 1990s and beyond to prevent respiratory distress and address certain cardiac problems.

Medical costs for neonatal treatment of low birth weight babies averaged $30,000 in 2000. Ongoing treatment for the 30% who suffer severe impairments, amortized over all low birth weight babies has a net present value average of about $40,000 more. So we average spending about $70,000 more for low birth weight babies today than we did in the 1950s.

What do we get in return? Mortality has fallen for low birth weight babies from about 18% in 1950 to about 5% today. Mortality for the smallest infant subcategory—those weighing under 2 lbs. at birth—has fallen from about 90% in 1950 to about 40% today. Mortality in the next largest subcategory—babies weighing 2—3 lbs. at birth—has fallen from 55% in 1950 to 5% today.

Average life expectancy of low birth weight babies has increased by 15 years since 1950. Though difficult to measure objectively their quality of life, some 75% rated their health as 'excellent or nearly so' when surveyed by the Journal of the American Medical Association in 1996. This is largely a testament to medical advances in treating low birth weight complications.

Let's now value the benefits of this $70,000 investment. We have already assigned a $100,000 value to each additional year of life. Against this, we subtract the high social costs of special education for the impaired group—averaging about $10,000/low birth weight baby/year, for an additional life year gain of $90,000. We modify this by the 75% 'excellent or nearly so' survey factor and discount back to today at 3%.

Our formula becomes: 15 years x 75% x $90,000 = $1,000,000 benefit. Using a 3% discount factor, we have a Net Present Value of about $350,000. (13)

For every dollar invested in low birth weight baby treatment, we (the child and society) receive back about $5 of benefit. This is an extremely high return on our investment. Private industry would generally be satisfied with $1.20 return on a $1.00 investment and the government typically looks for $1.10.

Our investment in low birth weight baby medical intervention looks wise, positive and very worthwhile indeed. Based on the ROI, this medical intervention is 'not expensive.'

CASE STUDY: ANTI-DEPRESSIVE MEDICATIONS (14)

The US Surgeon General estimates that 10 million Americans suffer from major depression. Episodes may strike suddenly, may occur in response to trauma (death of a family member or work difficulties for example) or may build over time and turn from mild to major depression. Depressive episodes may last from weeks to months. Untreated, 50% of people suffering a first episode will have a recurrence with subsequent episodes becoming more common.

The American Psychiatric Association has defined a set of diagnostic standards for depression. To be diagnosed as depressed a person must exhibit 5 or more of the following symptoms nearly everyday during a 2-week period, and this must mark a change from previous behavior. At least one symptom must be either a depressed mood or loss of interest or pleasure.

1. Depressed mood most of the day
2. Diminished interest or pleasure in all, or most, activities
3. Significant unintended weight loss or gain or an appetite change
4. Insomnia or hypersomnia
5. Psychomotor agitation or retardation
6. Fatigue or loss of energy
7. Feelings of worthlessness or excessive or inappropriate guilt
8. Diminished ability to think or concentrate or indecisiveness
9. Recurrent thoughts of death or suicide

The 1990 estimated costs of depression included $12 billion in direct medical costs plus significantly more indirect costs. These indirect costs include a reduced capacity to work or a student's reduced ability to attend to academic issues. Depression often strikes in the teens and 20's.

Treatment for depression includes a combination of drugs and psychotherapy. Doctors prescribe SSRIs or Selective Serotonin Reuptake Inhibitors, generally from the following list:

Prozac (approved by the FDA in 1987)
Zoloft (approved in 1992)
Paxil (approved in 1993)
Luvox (approved in 1994)
Celexa (approved in 1998).

Drugs similar to SSRIs include Wellbutrin (approved in 1985), Effexor (approved in 1993) and Serzone (approved in 1995). These medications have two prime advantages over previous drugs. First they have fewer side effects so can be tolerated by more people. Second, patients take these drugs at or near their effective levels. Older medications needed a longer ramp-up time. This requires fewer doctor visits to adjust the medications.

The average SSRI treatment per depressed person in 2000 cost about $600. This cost has remained roughly constant over time, for as medication patents run out people switch to lower cost generic drugs.

The primary benefit of treatment is an increase in individual happiness and good health, rather than an increase in life years. Valuing this benefit is difficult and the best method we have to measure this life quality is survey results.

Surveys indicate that people will make a time trade-off: when life with or without depression is described, people respond on average that they would be willing to accept 6 years without depression for 10 years of life with depression. This gives us a QALY improvement of $40,000/year for successful depression treatment. We discount this 10-year cash flow benefit stream by 3% for an annual improvement of about $32,500.

We make 3 additional adjustments. First, studies also indicate that SSRI treatment reduces the time spent depressed by about 10 weeks, so the actual annual successful treatment benefit per patient becomes about $6500. Second, studies indicate that 'undepressed' people work more productively and earn slightly more—about $600 per capita. Third, treatment is successful for only about 60% of patients taking SSRIs. (15) Thus the actual economic benefit per depression treatment nets around $4000 for the $600 investment—or almost $7 for every $1 invested. A very good return.

CASE STUDY: CARDIOVASCULAR DISEASE (16)

Since 1950 the US cardiovascular disease mortality rate has fallen by over half. Cardiovascular medical treatment today includes a variety of intensive procedures and medications. Physicians prescribe blood thinners to reduce the chance of blood clots, thrombolytic drugs to dissolve blood clots and beta-blockers to reduce the heart workload. Surgeries include cardiac catheterization (developed in 1959), coronary artery bypass graft (developed in 1968), and angioplasty (developed in 1978). Wire mesh stents, developed in the 1990s are often used to keep arteries clear of plaque build-up.

Non-acute medications, including antihypertensives to control blood pressure, cholesterol-lowering drugs and diabetes management drugs help prevent heart attacks, as do behavioral changes such as stopping smoking, improved diet and increased exercise. As a result, mortality from heart attacks has fallen by 75% since the 1950s. We have also had a 25% reduction in the percentage of our population that develop serious cardiovascular disease today as compared to 1950.

Today's 45 year old can expect to spend $30,000 (present value) on cardiac disease treatment over his or her remaining years of life. This same 45 year old can expect to live 4.5 years longer than his or her counterpart of 1950 almost entirely because cardiovascular disease mortality has decreased. Roughly 2/3 of this benefit, or 3 years, comes directly from medical treatment improvements, according to Cutler's analysis.

Three additional life years x $90,000/year give a discounted benefit value of about $120,000. This is substantially greater than the $30,000 cost yielding about $4 in benefits for every $1 invested—a very good return.

WHAT DOES THIS MEAN?

Our analysis showing excellent economic returns on our healthcare investment upends the healthcare debate. In previous chapters we looked at ways to control healthcare spending, to reduce the amount of GDP going to healthcare and to limit the resources we invest in healthcare. Our discussion of indemnity insurance and managed care shared a financial objective: to maintain (if not improve) healthcare quality while cutting costs. Association health plans and health savings accounts were designed to control healthcare costs. The British NHS case study showed some effects of constraining healthcare spending.

All these financial control methods share an underlying economic objective: to shift spending from healthcare to other economic activities. The underlying assumption: we—American consumers and public spenders—can get higher economic returns by purchasing other (non-healthcare) goods and services.

But in this chapter we have seen that at least some healthcare interventions provide a <u>higher economic return</u> than investments in many other fields. If this is right, then it DOES NOT make sense to limit our healthcare investments—for the ROI we obtain from purchasing other goods and services is often LOWER than our healthcare ROI. Indeed, based on this chapter's argument, we may currently spend TOO LITTLE on healthcare, not too much.

Economists Robert Hall of Stanford University and Charles Jones of Berkeley have pushed this idea even further. (17) They postulate that as people get richer, the relative value of additional material purchases decreases. Which, they ask, is more valuable—a third car, another television, more clothing—or an extra year of life? They suggest that for wealthier folks the most valuable consumption choice is to purchase additional life years. Indeed, they suggest that 'the value of life grows roughly twice as fast as income.'

This helps explain why we prefer to invest in expensive new technologies rather than in lower cost treatments—our third definition of moral hazard. The most obvious explanation, according to these authors: 'new and expensive technologies are valued because of the rising value of life.'

This raises an interesting social welfare investment question. As our baby boomers age and get wealthier, and as their consumption trends more toward healthcare, how much <u>should</u> our society spend on healthcare? Hall and Jones suggest that optimal US health spending should rise and that future increases in health spending are economically desirable. They conclude:

> We believe it likely that maximizing social welfare in the United States will require the development of institutions that are consistent with spending **30 percent or more of GDP** on health by the middle of the century. (Emphasis added.)

Perhaps they are right—that the ROI in American healthcare really exceeds the return on most other investments. And perhaps we can now begin to answer the question that opened this chapter: Is American healthcare expensive or not? The answer, according to Hall, Jones, Cutler and others may well be 'not.'

WHERE IS MORAL HAZARD?

We have seen that at least some investments in the US healthcare system yield high, positive returns on investment. These investments—in low birth weight babies, anti-depressive medications and cardiovascular care—are not terribly 'expensive' because we get such high returns. From an economic viewpoint (though not necessarily a cash-flow viewpoint) our <u>actual</u> healthcare expenditures are less important than our healthcare <u>return on investment</u>—if that is high, we make good economic choices by investing in healthcare.

We have uncovered a dilemma. On one hand specific healthcare interventions show very high returns on investment. On the other hand, our healthcare system suffers from widespread waste—some 30% according to various Dartmouth medical school economists. Though we have high ROIs from specific investments, we may have a poor systemic ROI. This chapter's discussion focused only on specific medical treatments rather than viewing the entire the US medical system.

We turn in our final chapter to a wider view. We will look at programs designed to replicate the high ROI from some medical treatments while reducing unnecessary or inappropriate interventions. These programs seek not necessarily to <u>eliminate</u> moral hazard from healthcare (by, for example, completely overhauling our healthcare finance system and switching to a single payer system), but rather to <u>reduce</u> systemic waste. Doing so, claim advocates, will save money, improve healthcare outcomes and raise our overall healthcare ROI while continuing to maintain the widespread consumer choice that currently defines our healthcare system.

Chapter 6: Notes

1. This chapter is a summary of David M. Cutler, 'Your Money or Your Life', Oxford University Press, 2004, which provided both

the framework and examples. All summary and interpretive errors are mine.

2. Cutler uses American economic values for this analysis for a number of reasons. First, our estimates are all in US dollars and this avoids any international currency issues. Second, all Americans (arguably) share certain socio-cultural values that may differ from other countries. Third, our consumption examples are American based and may not apply elsewhere.

3. There is a similar methodology called 'willingness to accept' that looks at how much people need to be compensated to accept a greater health risk. This would try to measure, for example, how much someone would need to be paid to promise never to have by-pass surgery. This may be methodologically more difficult to measure.

4. This methodology assumes that we can discover 'average' American values by measuring aggregate consumption decisions. Clearly some peoples' preferences deviate from the average—by definition. For example, some people might wish to invest more in medical intervention for children, based on the lengthy prospective payback period. Others might wish to invest more in the elderly as a reward for previous contributions to society. Or others might not be as enthusiastic about providing medical treatment for people whose behavior caused their medical condition—smokers, for example. But the 'willingness to pay' methodology offers two attractive features. First, data are relatively easily available; second, aggregating thousands or millions of consumption decisions seems to show consistent behavior patterns.

5. These data come from John D. Graham, et al, "The Cost-Effectiveness of Air Bags by Seating Position," Journal of the American Medical Association 278, no. 17 (November 5, 1997): 1418-25.

6. 2000 US Census estimate

7. Technically we should discount the future value of life years back to their present value. When doing this, use a very low discount rate as from routine investments like US bonds or bank CDs. This is because most people will never have their

life saved by an air bag so will continue with their routine lives.

8. 'Willingness to pay' analysis provides ballpark, rather than exact economic values. For our purposes such ballpark figures suffice, for we only want to see if healthcare investments—with the encumbrance of moral hazard—offer positive or negative returns.

9. 'Where Now for Saving Lives?' R. Zeckhauser and D. Shepard, Law and Contemporary Problems 40, No. 4 (1976): 5-45.

10. In spite of the quantitative and methodological problems, 'QALY theory is the most thoroughly worked approach to cost effectiveness analysis' in healthcare according to ETHOX at the University of Oxford ('Cost-effectiveness analysis (CEA) and QALY theory', ETHOX: University of Oxford found at **www. ethox.org.uk**).

Some University of Wisconsin researchers have ranked medical treatments by QALY (see Wisconsin Public Health and Health Policy Institute, May 26, 2005, unpublished paper by Gold, et al, located at **www. pophealth.wisc.edu/uwphi/publications/forums/wisconsin529.ppt**)

Condition or Treatment	Cost per QALY
Erectile Dysfunction	$6,400/QALY
Physician Counseling for Smoking	$7,200/QALY
Total Hip Replacement	$9,900/QALY
Gastric Bypass Surgery	$20,000/QALY
Osteoporosis Treatment	$38,000/QALY
Diabetes Control	$154,000/QALY
Left Ventricular Assist Device	$900,000/QALY

11. Cutler, page 18

12. Cutler, pages 22—31

13. These are Cutler's numbers. Cutler makes another quality of life adjustment for the high rate of low birthweight babies who require on-going medical assistance, reducing the QALY from 15 to 13 years. This has little bearing on the ROI estimate. See Cutler, pages 25—27.

14. For details on this analysis, see Cutler, pages 32—46.

15. Researchers have a difficult time determining the accuracy of

depression diagnosis. Physicians sometimes miscategorize their patients, either by error or potentially to avoid a depression-diagnosis stigma for their patients. See Cutler, pages 134-5, note #30. Some studies indicate that 40% of patients may take SSRIs for conditions other than depression.

16. Cutler, pages 47—60
17. Robert E. Hall and Charles I. Jones 'The Value of Life and the Rise in Health Spending', April 7, 2006, version 5.0 to be published in the Quarterly Journal of Economics

CHAPTER 7
Some Hope for the Future

What have we learned so far?

First, healthcare is fundamentally different from other forms of economic activity, and moral hazard accounts for perhaps 1/3 of our healthcare expenditures.

Second, consumers have consistently demanded wider provider access with less carrier interference.

Third, providers can adjust to, modify or skirt many cost control regulations.

Fourth, single payer systems—using Britain as an example—offer unattractive solutions to our moral hazard problems.

Fifth, we still get a good positive return on our healthcare investment, despite the moral hazard waste.

President Bush has been unable to design programs that satisfy American consumers and control healthcare costs. Medicare and Medicaid have been similarly unable to control costs adequately. Perhaps we have been looking too hard in the wrong places for solutions to our healthcare problems.

We have been looking for structural solutions—managed care versus indemnity coverage, health savings accounts versus managed care or single payer systems versus our current managed competition—rather than focusing on specific incremental steps to improve our healthcare delivery system. Perhaps we can take a series of incremental steps to improve healthcare quality and thereby decrease need for unnecessary medical treatments—often that simply correct prior substandard medical care.

In this chapter we will look at some new ways to improve our healthcare quality—and in the process reduce some moral hazard systemic waste. Rather than taking a revolutionary approach—for example, designing a brand new form of healthcare or switching to a single payer system—this chapter will modestly outline ways to reduce moral hazard waste...and save thousands of lives and billions of dollars in the process. As we take this approach, we aim to retain the many good aspects of US healthcare—rapid introduction of new technologies, short waits for treatment and wide access to providers—while we improve healthcare quality for most Americans.

Moral hazard infects our healthcare system by promoting inefficiencies. These come primarily from consumers demanding excessive treatment and providers acquiescing. This results, as we have argued, are extraordinarily high American healthcare costs and only average (compared to other First World countries) healthcare outcomes.

In this chapter I propose a three-step approach to addressing this problem. Step 1 addresses the problem of our healthcare uninsureds. Step 2 aims to improve medical treatment efficiency. And Step 3 focuses on improving our healthcare systemic customer service.

STEP 1: INSURING THE UNINSURED

We have a very high number of uninsured people—perhaps 15% of our population. These people access healthcare for which others (sometimes the government, but often the privately insured) pay with excess insurance premiums. The uninsured fall outside our normal managed healthcare system of low cost preventive care that (hopefully) avoids high cost emergency treatment. Our uninsured population has notoriously high healthcare costs and poor healthcare results.

The Institute of Medicine noted (1) that working age Americans without health insurance are more likely to:

- Receive too little medical care and receive it too late;
- Be sicker and die sooner;
- Receive poorer care when they are hospitalized.

These people often go without appropriate care. For example, the uninsured more often

- Go without cancer screening tests thus delaying diagnoses;
- Do not receive care recommended for chronic diseases, like timely eye and foot exams to prevent blindness and amputations in people with diabetes;

- Lack regular access to medications to managed conditions such as hypertension;
- Receive fewer diagnostic and treatment services after a traumatic injury or heart attack.

The IOM summarizes its findings as

'The health and length of life of working-age Americans would improve if they obtained coverage…they would use preventive services more often and would be less likely to delay seeking care, thus making early detection and treatment of problems more feasible.'

The uninsured contribute to our medical system inefficiencies with all three types of moral hazard. First, they may get care worth less than what it costs—for emergency room visits are much more expensive than physician office visits. (2) Second, their care is much more expensive than their PCP would recommend, for they have no PCP to guide them through the healthcare maze. And third, they receive little or no access to low cost or preventive treatments.

Some states, particularly Massachusetts and California, have begun experimenting with programs to expand health coverage to all residents. The Massachusetts plan enacted in 2006 includes both employer and individual mandates. All Massachusetts's businesses with 11+ employees must offer health insurance and all state residents must have health coverage or pay fines. Massachusetts will phase this program into existence. During its first year of operation the only penalty for individuals who fail to obtain health coverage is loss of their personal income tax exemption. In years two and three, penalties increase to include the personal exemption loss plus a fine equal to half the price of health insurance.

The Commonwealth knows that treating the uninsured costs approximately $1.3 billion annually. (3) This money is fairly inefficiently spent on expensive emergency care and poor preventive and primary care. Massachusetts will divert some of this 'free care' money to subsidize health insurance for low-moderate income uninsured state residents, thus bringing them under the health insurance umbrella and offering them access to more appropriate services. Here is the approximate breakdown by income of the uninsured Massachusetts's population in 2006:

Total Massachusetts population.................................	6,200,000
Currently insured (93%)...	5,830,000
Currently uninsured (7%).......................................	370,000
Uninsured earning under 100% of Federal Poverty Level....	70,000
Uninsured earning between 100 – 300% of FPL...............	140,000
Uninsured earning 300%+ of the FPL...........................	160,000

Massachusetts will subsidize health coverage for the approximately 210,000 residents earning up to 300% of the Federal Poverty Level—$29,412 for individuals and $60,012 for families of 4 people in 2006.

Massachusetts hopes that by end-year 3, most (if not all) of the uninsured residents will have health coverage. The goal is better, more efficient and more effective medical treatment for these 370,000 people. This program is being studied by many other states that hope to learn from the Massachusetts experience and implement similar activities.

STEP 2: ADDRESSING HEALTHCARE TREATMENT INEFFICIENCIES

American hospital treatment is notoriously inefficient. Commentators estimate, for example that a fifth of congestive-heart-failure patients are readmitted within a month of leaving the hospital; half are readmitted within a year. If patients were better managed, up to half of these readmissions could be prevented. (4)

According to the Institute of Medicine (5) preventable medical errors cost the US economy between $17 billion and $29 billion annually plus thousands of preventable annual deaths. These errors include diagnostic, treatment, preventive and systemic problems. The IOM believes that faulty systems, processes and conditions, rather than individual physician mistakes cause these medical errors.

The National Committee on Quality Assurance (NCQA)—a managed care industry association—has picked up on the IOM work and has designed a system to measure healthcare quality in great detail. The NCQA calls itself the 'watchdog for the managed care industry' (6) and reports medical treatment outcomes in it's HEDIS model (below).

Note an interesting data-gathering evolutionary process. During the 1970s and 80s, many of our current medical technologies and treatments were just being invented. Researchers lacked access to medical outcome data over long time periods. Also, the lack of integration among medical funding sources has made reporting objective data difficult—carriers, hospitals and physicians sometimes had different motivations for releasing information, and may have released only partial information (if they provided any data at all). By contrast, the NCQA reports extensive, objective data as a requirement of carrier affiliation. The NCQA data does not suffer from the problems that plagued previous data-based measurement programs.

Addressing Healthcare Treatment Inefficiencies: HEDIS

The **HEALTH PLAN EMPLOYER DATA AND INFORMATION SET** (HEDIS) measures healthcare system performance using over 60 different measures of treatment and service. HEDIS data are collected over a very wide cross-section of the healthcare marketplace and are very specifically defined (unlike the PSRO data or treatment guidelines in Chapters 2 and 3). This allows the NCQA to compare performance of managed care plans and medical treatments on an 'apples-to-apples' basis, and to make very specific recommendations.

Why do health plans and providers report their data to the NCQA? Several reasons, primarily related to customer service and marketing. Health plans want to report their compliance with HEDIS standards to the public and receive NCQA accreditation—something highly valued in the managed care community. Plans also want their national NCQA rankings, published annually in US News and World Report, to showcase their excellence.

Providers want to inform the public of their outstanding work. Some health plans rank providers by HEDIS compliance and offer these rankings to the public. Providers all want to appear at the top of this list and failure to appear on the list at all may raise patient/consumer concerns.

Some major NCQA observations (7):

The 'disparity between the care most Americans receive and the care delivered through the nation's best plans results in from 42,000 to 79,000 premature deaths each year.'

GARY FRADIN

There are 'thousands of preventable second heart attacks, kidney failures and other conditions...more than $9 billion in lost productivity and nearly $2 billion in hospital costs could be averted through more consistent delivery of best-practice care...more than 14,000 heart attacks and strokes could be prevented each year through better diabetes management alone'

The 2004 NCQA report quantified some potential direct medical expense savings by closing the quality gap. Here are examples:

Measure	Avoidable Events/Year	Cost Savings
Breast Cancer Screening	7600 treatments in Stage IV due to late diagnosis	$48 Million
Colorectal Cancer Screenings	20,000 cases diagnosed/treated at later stage	$191 Million
Controlling High Blood Pressure	16,000 major cardio events (e.g. heart attacks)	$463 Million
Appropriate Diabetes Care	14,000 heart attacks, strokes or amputations	$573 Million

The 2004 Report also estimated the avoidable annual deaths attributable to unexplained variations in care. For example:

Issue	Avoidable Deaths
Beta Blocker Treatment after Coronary	900 – 1900
Controlling High Blood Pressure	15,000 – 26,000
Colorectal Cancer Screening	4,200 – 6,300
Flu Shots for Over 65s	3,500 – 7,300

This quality focus and adoption of 'best practices' nationally could generate enormous savings. Providers could treat patients correctly the first time—and eliminate many subsequent doctor visits and hospitalizations. Here are some potential provider quality improvements:

Condition	National Baseline	90th percentile	Spread
Advising smokers to quit	59%	76%	17%
Beta Blocker use after coronary	86%	100%	14%
Cervical Cancer Screening	82%	88%	6%
Timely Pre-Natal Care	81%	96%	15%
Controlling High Blood Pressure	49%	71%	22%

As providers improve to the 90th percentile practices we will save lives and resources. In effect, the NCQA has redefined good healthcare quality and systemic efficiency to mean '90th percentile (or better) practices'.

102

This is very different from the Professional Standard Review Organizations and the Professional Review Organizations. Neither had the rich national data available to the NCQA from the HEDIS effort. Both PSROs and PROs focused on providers who operated outside a treatment norm, rather than measuring providers against an objective, outcome based set of treatment protocols. (8)

The 2005 NCQA Annual Report praised Elliott Fisher and others at Dartmouth for highlighting the inverse relationship between spending and quality. The Report quotes Fisher that 'more care isn't necessarily better care. In fact, everything suggests that it is slightly the opposite: the higher cost systems have worse outcomes.' Fisher found that

> There is not enough spending in high-cost regions on thing like preventive care or proven treatments for heart attack patients. At the same time, patients who undergo more tests, treatment and hospital stays are inevitably exposed to more risks. Eliminating unnecessary care eliminates some of the harm that is an inevitable side effect of care.

HEDIS and the NCQA take direct aim at the moral hazards of (1) receiving care worth less than its longevity or life quality benefits and (2) ignoring less expensive treatments in favor of more expensive treatments. In short, the HEDIS model provides a roadmap to maximizing the ROI from our healthcare investment.

How does the NCQA suggest we modify our healthcare system to focus on valuable, efficient and necessary treatment? The short answer: by convincing carriers (including Medicare and Medicaid) to pay providers based on their performance, not just based on their activity levels. As the NCQA (2005 Report) quotes Dolores L. Mitchell, Executive Director of the Massachusetts Group Insurance Commission, 'procedure X is rewarded no matter how well or poorly it is done...we have got to...make some qualitative judgements about performance.'

Addressing Healthcare Treatment Inefficiencies:
Pay for Performance

The 'Pay for Performance' concept is quite simple: offer financial incentives to providers who give high quality medical service. HEDIS defines 'high quality medical service' at its 90th percentile level and provides a credible, data-based, national guideline for providers to follow.

There were 35 Pay for Performance programs in 2003, 75 by mid-2004 and 150+ by early 2005, primarily in the private sector. (9) There are currently over 100 other demonstration projects underway nationally. (10) Three major American medical societies—the American Medical Association, American Academy of Family Physicians and the Medical Group Management Association—and the Centers for Medicare & Medicaid Services and the Institute of Medicine all support the Pay for Performance concept and have recommended principles.

Medicare has 3 noteworthy large Pay for Performance demonstration projects currently underway. The first 'Hospital Quality Initiatives' provides a negative incentive (4/10 of 1% of Medicare payments withheld) to hospitals that simply do not report on 10 quality measures. The result: 98.3% report. Medicare hopes to use this data when designing future performance based bonus programs.

Second, Medicare funds the 'Premier Hospital Quality Incentive Demonstration' that rewards hospitals demonstrating high-quality performance in acute care areas. To bonus, a hospital must be in the top percentage nationally in at least 1 of 5 areas: heart attack, heart failure, pneumonia, coronary artery bypass graft or hip and knee replacement. Performance is based on 34 quality indicators. Hospitals in the top 10% nationally get a 2% Medicare bonus; hospitals in the next 10% get a 1% Medicare bonus.

Third, the 'Physician Group—Practice Demonstration' aims to improve coordination between Medicare Part A (hospital) and B (physician) services. This program promotes investment in administrative structures and processes and rewards physicians for improving health outcomes. Physician groups can also earn Medicare performance based bonuses as they achieve savings compared to a control group.

According to Mark McClellan Administrator for the Centers for Medicare & Medicaid Services:

> Until recently, about 95 percent of Medicare spending went to treating health problems after they happen—paying for the emergency room, putting you in the hospital, or doing surgery when something goes wrong...But it doesn't have to be that way...by anticipating patient

needs, especially patients with chronic diseases, healthcare teams—in partnership with patients—(we) can intervene before expensive procedures and hospitalizations are required...(11)

The American Academy of Actuaries urges some notes of caution about Pay for Performance models. The Academy has expressed concern about bonus programs that induce providers to follow the HEDIS or other guidelines; small bonuses may not affect sufficient behavioral change, and large bonuses need very careful study. (12) Also, Pay for Performance provider bonuses are payable in the near term, while most healthcare cost reductions come in the future. This creates a potential financial bind. The exact Pay for Performance structure will evolve over time as our healthcare system gains experience implementing this relatively new concept.

One specific non-Medicare Pay for Performance initiative is the Bridges to Excellence (BTE) program, launched by a coalition of US employers with help from the American Diabetes Association and American Heart Association/American Stroke Association, that ties provider compensation to performance in diabetes, cardiovascular and stroke treatment. Studies have shown that program physicians offered care 'substantially more consistent with best practice guidelines'. These physicians also delivered care at a 10—15% lower cost than non-participating physicians did. Most savings come from reduced hospitalization frequency, both inpatient and emergency room. (13)

The NCQA notes a number of other quality-based initiatives undertaken by specific health insurers. All aim to reduce systemic inefficiencies discussed throughout this book. Here are some creative examples (14):

Improve Office Technologies. Currently, only about 31% of hospital emergency rooms, 29% of outpatient departments and 17% of doctors' offices have electronic medical records that support patient care. The Computerized Physician Order Entry (CPOE) system can compare a prescription order against normal dosing standards, check for allergies or drug interactions and warn of potential patient problems. Currently only about 8% of physicians use CPOE.

Interestingly, both Kaiser and the US Veterans Health Administration system use computers for electronic health records, CPOE, lab test results, imaging studies and clinical reminders. Not coincidentally, both Kaiser and the VA score highly on the HEDIS scales.

The VA, in particular, estimates that 96% of all it's prescription and medical orders are now entered electronically, compared to the national average of 8%. That improves efficiency. 'One out of five tests in a civilian hospital have to be repeated because the paper results are lost' estimates Veterans Affairs Secretary R. James Nicholson. 'That's not happening in our hospitals.' (15)

Electronic Patient Registry. Minnesota-based HealthPartners uses a creative 'team approach' to patient care. An electronic patient registry and electronic medical records system provide information about which patients need certain tests, screenings or preventive visits.

For example, a medical assistant reviews records of patients with cardiac disease, chronic pain, diabetes or stroke—all known to increase patient risk of depression—prior to an appointment to see if they are due for a depression screening. If so, a nurse administers the screening prior to the patient's visit with the doctor.

Bring All Your Medications. Minnesota-based Medica mails a brown lunch bag once each year to all patients over age 55 who take five or more regular medications (about 19,000 members). On the bag is a sticker asking the patient to bring all his or her medications—including over-the-counter medications such as vitamins and herbal supplements—to the next doctor's visit for a 'medication check-up.'

'This program has several benefits', according to Kristina Bloomquist, the brown bag project clinical manger in 2004. 'It helps us make sure that patients are taking their medications correctly, that they aren't taking expired medications or drugs that interact badly, and that generic brands are considered when appropriate.' An added value of having all medications reviewed by one provider is the opportunity to coordinate dosage schedules in a way that makes it easiest for patients to follow.

Though the direct cost of this program is quite small, the value in terms of improved patient compliance and safety is potentially quite large. Note how this program deviates from the common practice of Miami Medicare recipients outlined in Chapter 1. A common, anecdotal complaint of elderly Floridians is that they can't keep their medications straight. Their moral hazard behavior helps lead to that problem. Minnesota's Medica aims to help solve that problem, but also requires more Primary Care Provider involvement and imposes restrictions on specialist visits. (I wonder how the Miami Medicare recipients would accept that.)

Wallet Cards for Diabetes Patients. Harvard Pilgrim Health Care in Massachusetts provides diabetes patients with a wallet card containing 7 questions they should ask at every doctor's visit. 'These are key messages that remind both patients and providers about the importance of routinely checking cholesterol and blood pressure, taking a daily aspirin, and getting a regular eye and foot exam' says Judith Frampton, Harvard's Vice President of Clinical Quality Programs. 'By educating our members we are also driving physician behavior.'

Electronic Medical Records. Kaiser Permanente Health Plan in California is rolling out a $3 billion information system to allow every doctor in the system full access to patient medical records. This will allow physicians to order tests, write prescriptions and make referrals via computer. When fully installed in 2007, the system will connect all Kaiser facilities, including hospitals, medical office buildings, labs and pharmacies. 'If a member arrives in the emergency room of any of our hospitals, the staff will be able to access his or her medical record' says Louise Liang, Senior Vice President for Quality and Clinical Support Systems.

Kaiser customers can view their own medical records on a secure website and can also make appointments, look up lab tests and prescriptions and find links to health information related to their needs. This system 'empowers patients to participate more fully in their care,' according to Liang.

Interestingly, patients with better access to their own medical information feel more empowered and have reduced demands for wider and easier access to specialists and other providers. Patients demand this wide access (in part) because they feel unempowered…hopefully empowered patients will have less need to abuse the healthcare system. (See below).

Setting Goals Together. Patients at Group Health Cooperative in Seattle are full partners in their care. Group Health helped create the Shared Care Plan, a paper- and computer-based self-management tool that helps patients create a personalized health record to track information about their health, including their symptoms, treatments, medications, tests and personal goals. The Shared Care Plan was designed in response to patient requests for more control over their medical information.

Research shows that patients are more successful at changing behaviors when they are involved in setting their goals according to the NCQA. Goal setting participation is one way to empower patients.

Patient Consideration. The US Veterans Administration has adopted a 'Sorry Now' program to transform its hospitals from unaccountable bureaucracies to a more patient friendly environment. In 2005 the VA instituted a systemwide policy of apologizing for medical or customer service errors. In every department of the Buffalo VA hospital, for example, hang posters with the name, photo and phone number of the supervisor, inviting patients to call with questions or complaints. The Buffalo hospital also wants to limit patient waiting room times to 15 minutes. And after every outpatient visit and inpatient release, a staffer follows up with a phone call to the patient, to ensure that there are no problems. 'They've adopted a culture of patient safety and quality that is pervasive' says Karen Davis, president of the Commonwealth Fund that studies healthcare issues. (16)

STEP THREE: IMPROVING HEALTHCARE CUSTOMER SERVICE

Our healthcare system has failed to keep current with customer service technologies and practices currently used by other industries. Bank customers, for example, commonly have 24/7 electronic or ATM access to their money without need to visit a bank physically during office hours. This saves the bank money and improves customer satisfaction. But chronically ill healthcare customers must still visit a medical facility for even the simplest test. This is very costly: the patient must transport him/herself to the facility and the facility pays labor and overhead costs for the tester—analogous to banking many years ago. Our current technologies should allow patients to take simple tests at home and upload results to their physician.

Hungry food consumers can order and receive a hot pizza within 30 minutes, but not a prescription from their local pharmacy. Why not? (17)

Computers remind us to pay our bills but not take our medications. Cars tell us when some automotive system is 'out-of-specification', but our medical system does not. Dentists and veterinarians commonly send our appointment reminder notices but primary care physicians do not.

We could use information technology more advantageously. Computers could monitor physician prescriptions, patient medication rates and medication interactions to reduce physician error. Computers could also send patients email reminders to take prescriptions or to have diagnostic tests. Current information technology can allow for remote monitoring of patients to ensure that they're taking their medications, to monitor their conditions…and if conditions change, to inform the doctor.

Computer technology could also reduce duplication that is pervasive in our healthcare system. Many chronically ill patients take the same tests for different physicians or forget to bring test results to appointments. Computers could replace our antiquated paper-based reporting systems and improve healthcare quality while saving money.

Patients complain that our medical system is not 'user-friendly' and that they feel unempowered. Perhaps initiatives like Group Health Cooperative's 'Setting Goals Together' and the VA's 'Sorry Now' will help make patients feel more empowered and more trusting of their medical providers and organizations.

These are among a host of incremental steps currently pursued by various health carriers and providers to increase our medical systemic efficiency. Some of these ideas will work, others will not. But improving our healthcare systemic customer service and efficiency will address the three moral hazards described in our Introduction.

First more patients will <u>receive care worth at least what it costs</u>. The NCQA Best Practice guidelines will help providers practice good preventive medicine and reduce the number of unnecessary hospital re-admissions. Some of these innovative customer service practices will reduce the number of medical errors and help consumers access better preventive treatment.

We also hope that these systemic improvements will induce consumers to trust both their physicians and our healthcare system more than currently. If our Miami Medicare elders (from Chapter 1) trusted their PCP to provide 'best practices' then they may have less need to self-refer to additional specialists. Indeed, if all Miami specialists had easy access to patient data, then the need for duplicate and surpurfluous tests would be reduced. The moral hazard demand for excess, unnecessary treatment—i.e. treatment where benefits are less than the costs—may go down.

Our second type of moral hazard—patients receiving treatment in excess of what their PCP would recommend absent financial considerations—would also go down. Indeed, the NCQA Best Practice guidelines are the treatment protocols that good PCPs should embrace.

Our third moral hazard—recommendation of the most rather than least expensive treatments—might also get modified. Good preventive medicine will help providers address smaller, less expensive medical problems through better screening for example, rather than waiting for a severe medical problem to emerge.

WILL THESE THREE STEPS REDUCE MORAL HAZARD?

This is clearly an evolutionary process. Supporters of the HEDIS/ Pay for Performance programs argue that we need additional time for data collection and analysis, technological development and pay for performance experience. Hopefully over time, these programs will contribute to healthcare quality improvements and cost controls.

Skeptics wonder about this. Other payment/treatment control methods looked attractive initially but failed to achieve their goals:

- Prospective Payment Systems were blunt instruments, soon replaced with Diagnosis Related Groups
- DRGs aimed at controlling costs, but spawned the for-profit hospital movement;
- Utilization Review became 'admit/don't admit' decisions with as many detractors as supporters;
- Treatment Guidelines attempted to promote uniform treatments, but guideline proliferation allowed physicians to ignore them.

Are HEDIS Best Practice guidelines and Pay for Performance ideas finally the Holy Grail of US medical practice? Or is this just another attempt to control the uncontrollable medical system that as evolved in this country?

Only time will tell.

But we have, perhaps, uncovered a middle road between the positions described at the end of Chapter 1. Goodman, Musgrave and Herrick (18) argued that regulations have suppressed the market mechanism in American healthcare, resulting in the huge inefficiencies described in this book. I think they are wrong. We need regulation—both governmental and industry self-policing—to protect consumers in this most complex of consumer-economic fields.

A laissez-faire approach might reduce moral hazard. Remember that moral hazard is defined as 'behavior changes due to insurance coverage'. Less generous insurance coverage for some—resulting from less regulation of healthcare—might well cost less. But as we saw in our analysis of President Bush's Association Health Plan proposal, less regulation will likely also lead to consumer confusion. Which plans pay for 'all' treatment, and which only for 'all allowable' treatment? I believe that the resulting consumer confusion—and the economic hardships likely endured by those purchasing inadequate coverage—outweigh the costs of our current level of regulation. I think that the price we pay for clarity and wide range of mandated coverage included in our private healthcare coverage—i.e. moral hazard—is justified.

I also disagree with Professors Fein and Richmond (and many others) who advocate single payer systems. (19) As argued in Chapter 5, American consumers will not accept the constraints on choice and treatment evident in Britain. Indeed, I argue that adoption of a single payer system in America would virtually inevitably lead to a re-creation of our current employer based health insurance system.

I hope that the NCQA/HEDIS model will help us reduce healthcare systemic inefficiencies. I also hope that our Pay for Performance experiments will show ways to keep our healthcare system relatively consumer responsive while reducing waste. I think both of these efforts offer promise for the future, and that both will need to evolve.

And finally, I hope that American healthcare consumers understand the excellent features of our system—including widespread access to top-notch providers and short waits for treatment. As our system evolves, I hope and expect that we will reduce our moral hazard waste while retaining the best aspects of our current healthcare system.

Chapter 7: Notes

1.   Institute of Medicine, Care without Coverage, May, 2002
2.   The average Massachusetts physician office visit in 2005 cost about $70, while the average emergency room visit cost about $550. Thus someone using the ER for routine care would need to get about $480 more value (however value is calculated) from this visit than from an office visit.

Note also Wennberg's claims in Chapter 1 that many ER activities are directed toward maintaining short term survival and do little to improve life quality or longevity. This can make an emergency room visit even less valuable.

3.   Data in this paragraph provided by the Massachusetts Healthcare Connector, lecture by Jon Kingsdale, December 18, 2006 at the Burlington (Massachusetts) Marriott Hotel.
4.   'A Supply Side Approach to Health Care', Karen Davis, Seattle Times, October 13, 2005
5.   Institute of Medicine, 'To Err is Human' 1999
6.   This claim and the next paragraph come from the NCQA website, **www.ncaq.org**
7.   These come from the 2004 NCQA Quality Report
8.   HEDIS relies on data provided by managed care organizations nationally and has become the 'gold standard in measuring and improving quality in managed care organizations' (2005 NCQA Annual Report). The HEDIS data collected through 2005, for example, come from carriers insuring 65 million people—a very broad cross-section of the US population and medical treatments. PSROs and PROs relied either on less or narrower data—or both.
9.   Reported in American Academy of Actuaries Issue Brief on Pay for Performance, October 2005.
10. NCQA 2005 Annual Report
11. NCQA, 2005 Annual Report

12. American Academy of Actuaries, op.cit.

13. Ibid.

14. All examples come from the NCQA 2005 Annual Report, except where noted.

15. 'The Best Medical Care in the U.S.' BusinessWeek, July 17, 2006

16. Ibid. This example was reported in BusinessWeek.

17. Several of these examples come from David Cutler, 'Your Money or Your Life', page 69

18. Goodman, et al, 'Lives at Risk'

19. Richmond and Fein, 'The Healthcare Mess'

www.ingramcontent.com/pod-product-compliance
Lightning Source LLC
Chambersburg PA
CBHW051541170526
45165CB00002B/834